Super Singles, Activate!

Testimonies to Inspire and Uplift
the Single Woman

Edited by

Neely Terrell & Alexis "Fly" Jones

Super Singles, Activate! Testimonies to Inspire and Uplift the Single Woman

Quotations have been used from the Holy Bible.

Some names and identifying characteristics of certain individuals in this book have been changed in order to protect their privacy.

ISBN-13: 978-1456591649

ISBN-10: 1456591649

Printed in the United States of America

To all women who need encouragement.

CONTENTS

foreword

First, let me share my story. I celebrated my fortieth birthday a few years ago, have a master's degree in international affairs and development, have produced a public access television program, *Spoken Word Live*, have a church home, have traveled to the Motherland (the East and West coasts of Africa), and I am single. Never been married without children! And quite frankly, no one has ever proposed to me.

No sympathy, please. Author, Claudette E. Sims, helped me to recognize that not all women will get married in her book, *Don't Weep for Me*, 1985.

I am gainfully employed, financially in control, emotionally stable, spiritually charged, and physically intact—not bad on the eyes—so I am told. And, I have more than ten spices in my kitchen cabinets (I can cook).

I think I have heard it all – as far as being single goes. In my early 20s, I heard,

"Your standards are too high!" "The man for you isn't born yet."

My aunts would say, "You better hurry up and get married before you get too old." or "How's your love life?" Men say in amazement, "Why are you single?!" "Do you even like men?!" My girlfriend who is about 7 years younger than I said, "You're almost 40, what are you going to do?" And now, one aunt just says, "You better hurry up and get married!" or

"When are you going to get married?" Another aunt continues with, "How's your love life?"

I am sure you are familiar with the constant, almost embarrassing questions focused on and directed toward single women, especially after a certain age. Perhaps that is why so many women are settling for less than God's best, rushing to get married, contributing to the vicious cycle of divorce and single-parent households. In this book, you will find that there are more of us than you think. I am comfortable, confident, and convinced that one day my king will come. Yours will also!

Of course, being single is not easy. As a single, Christian woman with or without children, there are a myriad of challenges that you will encounter – car and home maintenance issues, employers thinking single women without children can work around the clock (you might even work ridiculous hours, trying to occupy time), baby- and dog-sitters, household chores, grocery shopping, etc. The single woman simply does not have a companion to share the load. She is socially positioned to be the superwoman: able to cook, clean, wash, bake, sex, work, and solve the problems of the world. Be assured that knowing God *always* makes the load lighter.

When you activate yourself toward greatness, magnifying your superior light, your journey as a super single sister will become more balanced and less of a juggling act. You will say no, live alone, and handle your singleness God's way. The Bible says it this way in 1 Corinthians 7: 34b; single women must be busy in the Lord. "She wants to be holy in body and spirit." You will not have to overcompensate with food, extra-activities, children or men to fill space in your life.

Over the years, I have realized that being single is not a curse. It is actually a blessing. During your time of singleness, you must seize the opportunity to develop to your full potential, become the best *you* that you can be.

1. Honor your body as your temple. Set standards and uphold them.

2. Heal yourself from your past hurts, disappointments and struggles.

3. Learn to love and trust yourself, allowing the power of God that lives in you to manifest.

4. Master your relationship with God.

It is then, that you will be prepared for the king that God has prepared for you. Queen, sister, friend, woman of God, understand that you are blessed in every stage of your life. Embrace this stage of singleness and activate your spirit to bring forth the dynamic, awesome and powerful sister that God has called for such a time as this. This is the way you activate your super single life. Maybe then, your king will arrive on your doorstep, ready to honor you as his queen in the castle. While you wait, activate!!

Brenda M. Tillman
Author of *Shades of Mandingo* and
Listen – Your Positive Inner Voice

Super Singles, Activate!

Please Note:
This book was compiled over the course of one year (2010-2011) and some writers have gotten coupled, engaged, or married. Some classifications have changed. Also, because great minds think alike, some scriptures have been repeated in the following stories.

su-per [soo-per] **sin-gle** [sing-guhl], *n.*

—*noun, singular*

unmarried person who has superior qualities that are stemmed directly from the power of God.

Classifications of Super Singles

free [free], *adj.*—
without a significant other

cou-pled [kuh-puhld], *adj.*—
in a romantic relationship

en-gaged [en-geyjd], adj.—
soon to be married

di-vorced [dih-vohrsd], adj.—
legally separated from spouse

wi-dowed [wi-dohd], adj.—
lost husband by death and has not remarried

What Is a Super Single?

By Neely Terrell, *Free*

"For, Whoever would love life and see good days must keep his tongue from evil and his lips from deceitful speech. He must turn from evil and do good; he must seek peace and pursue it."

-1 Peter 3:10-11

How can someone who has been single for so long continue to remain refreshed, faithful, and positive toward love? What becomes of the super single? What on earth is a super single?

If you have not been in a happy relationship for a long period of time and yearn, obviously or secretly, for a good man or woman to enter your life, you are a *super single*. If you have not been in a committed relationship for a while, this title belongs to you. *Super* can be used in a negative or positive context. In a negative light, it can mean that you have no hope in a relationship. You can pretty much forget it. You may as well put love out of your mind because it is not meant for you nor will you ever come close to it. You are embittered by the couples around you and you slightly despise their public displays of affection.

You are not completely bitter, but there is a little bitterness.

However, in a positive light, super means that you are outstanding, fantastic, superb, splendid, confident, attractive, selfless, and motivated. You are not often down about not having a significant other. You have high hopes that love will glide in your direction, but it is not your main focus. You are so busy with other endeavors that the thought of love is not your obsession. Yes, you may desire it, but the thought of romantic love does not depress you. Therefore, your mind is on the right track.

I used to call myself, and still do on occasions, a "super single." Sometimes, I mean it in a good way, while others, not so good. I tease myself in front of others to add flair to conversation, but I have learned that it only makes me feel downtrodden in the end. I didn't really feel upset about being single. I just wanted to fit in. I didn't want to be so faithful and hopeful around my peers. I didn't want to be a light. I wanted to be dim like everyone else in the circle. Although it is comfortable to blend in with other bitter people, it's not a wise thing to do. We are all accountable for our actions. If we know that God is the supplier of all things, we must not writhe in nonsense. To lower our mentality into thinking that we cannot have true love is not healthy. Whether through playful conversation or not, we truly do have to be careful of what we say over our lives.

You will be surprised at what you say or think about yourself that will affect your self-esteem. I thought that it was fun to tell others that I was a super single. I meant it in a negative context and figured that it would be a great conversation, but how did I know that it was not becoming a reality in my life? I was just joking, but was my joke that serious? Was my negativity a contribution to my prolonged singleness?

I have written this to say while it is fun to make carefree jokes about our personal lives, we have to think about our current situations. The older we become, the more wisdom we should attain. We are to keep ourselves faithful in what God can do. We must not entertain evil forces by saying that we may never have a man. It can seem like a cool conversation to have, but we have to be mindful of what comes out of our mouths. We shouldn't play so much when it comes to our heart's desires. If your desire is to have a relationship or get married, you must not continue to say that it may never happen. If you are truly serious and prayerful about love, God counts on you to speak it into existence and believe. Trust Him and remain optimistic toward love.

The Waiting Room

By Alexis "Fly" Jones, *Free*

"But they that wait upon the LORD shall renew their strength; they shall mount up with wings as EAGLES, they shall run, and not be weary; and they shall walk, and not faint."

-Isaiah 40:31

If you have studied the Book of Ruth, the Book of Esther in the Holy Bible, or even read the fairytale story of Cinderella, you will find an existing theme or a common denominator among all three stories. This "common denominator" that I subsequently ignored for years has led me to realize the answer, at least for me, in the obtainment of my mate.

Let me first say that my belief is that my future mate, whoever he is, has been predestined. He is ordained for me and I for him. However, my lack of patience with the Lord on his arrival resulted in damaged emotions that mostly could have been avoided. Unlike Cinderella, I had been the one running around searching for my prince charming to make the shoe fit!

Here's my story.

In the past, my relationships with men have been more like the "Adventures of a Broken Heart." My strong desire to have or find a mate led me to look at every man I dated as [possibly] the "one." When he ended up not being that, my disappointment ran deep.

Such a repetitive cycle of heartache caused me to repeatedly bandage up a bleeding heart, without ever receiving heart surgery. Better stated, self-medicating the wound without receiving the spiritual stitches necessary for true healing by the Master Physician.

To add insult to injury, my own choosing ended with a tendency to always attract men that were not "ready for a relationship." And if they were, I would often find myself trying to change or mold them into the men that I wanted them to be for me. That is, a man after God's own heart; a man that would cherish and adore me; a man that would just want ME; a man that I knew if I were to marry him, he would love me as Christ loves the church. I came up short every time.

So began the process of...settling.

Though I am intelligent, have a great career, am a believer, a church-goer, keep my looks up, don't consider myself to be shabby looking and all that jazz, it seemed as if these qualities were never enough to "keep a man."

My first real heartache happened when a man I had known since I was a teenager, confessed his love for me and asked me to be his wife. Due to his erroneous thoughts of my betrayal (which he later recognized was faulty), we ended our 3+ year relationship. He ended up engaged to someone else only a few short months later and married the following year. The news of his marriage left me heartbroken, which created feelings of rejection and abandonment.

I would eventually move on to meet guys that were not good for me and didn't treat me the best. I purposely ignored red flags and once remembered being told these words: "No man could ever love you."

If anything, I had some unexplainable desire to render love to those that were openly selfish, deceitful, or straight-up players. I stayed in these relationships since I saw potential in what these men could be. I sacrificed my own happiness by not receiving the love I wanted in return. Even when I told myself I deserved better, loneliness and the desire for a companion still dug deeper. Insecurities crept themselves into my thought life. When it didn't work out with a guy, or we fell out, I felt rejected and battled with the *What's Wrong with Me?* Syndrome.

After seeking advice from friends, I had come to the decision to just "have fun" and not be "so serious."

I entered into a couple of relationships that weren't one of any form of commitment. I allowed these men to whisper sweet nothings in my ear, while I held on and voiced my *feelings* with hopes that one would want to change their status and choose me. It was unwise.

For over a period of six months, I became the friend to a man that provided the benefits of a relationship, indulging in sin just to receive the companionship I strongly craved. These desperate actions only led to many nights of tears on my pillow and weeks of depression.

I was running out of patience and belief in true love and marriage. My friends were getting hitched left-and-right and I'd just come to terms and embraced the fact that single it would be for me. I began to try to focus more on my career. I continued to assist others to get my mind off of my singleness, whether it was volunteering, or encouraging others through the word of God.

One day, during one of my down moments, I received an email from my mother, who is also an ordained minister and single woman herself.

She said, "Alexis, while you have suffered and experienced heartfelt pain early on in life, your heart of love and capacity to love the unlovable at your own expense is a supernatural gift from God. Your misery is your ministry."

She continued, "You are strong and the joy of the Lord is your strength. You shine as bright as the morning sun in the darkest of circumstances. Many days you gave me hope and courage to press on toward the high mark in Jesus Christ. You bless my life and now, IT IS YOUR SEASON! FLY ALEXIS, FLY!"

Such a statement caused a burst of encouragement and needless to say, a light bulb to go off in my head. It was that very email from my mom that I thought, *Alexis...choose Him!*

"But seek first the kingdom of God and his righteousness, and all these things will be added to you." -Matthew 6:33

By me choosing *Him* and allowing God to choose *him*, I have been able to redirect my focus. My misery with men has become a testimonial for ministry and the purpose for *Super Singles, Activate!* Daily, I am learning to place the Lord first, that He may reign SUPERerior in my life. I have found my mission to be an encourager and witness to others of Jesus Christ and His healing power.

I no longer dwell on, *What's wrong with me?* or worry about seeking out my Prince Charming or if he will find me because I have found the common denominator! In all three stories of the Book of Ruth, the Book of Esther, and story of Cinderella, the theme remains the same...

The men found their wives.

The biblical blueprint has been set. "He who finds a wife, finds a good thing and obtains favor from the LORD" (Proverbs 18:22). Such revelation allows me to rejoice in the fact that through the direction of the Holy Spirit, my King will find me when the Lord sees fit. When Boaz found his Ruth, she was working in the field. Her focus was on serving her Lord, while Esther was in her season of purpose.

Now, I wouldn't be honest if I didn't say that sometimes I still ask God if my mate is around the corner, but while I'm in the waiting room, I find the security, companionship, healing, love, satisfaction, and peace in the presence of Christ and hold steadfast to his promises.

While in your singleness, I charge you to forgive past hurts, release any bitterness, and strive toward being concerned about the purpose that the Holy of Holies has birthed inside of you. Allow God the opportunity to give you beauty for ashes. Let Him restore and heal you in every area. Though the world likes to say that time heals all wounds, I'd like to say that Jesus heals all wounds, including the wounds of the heart:

"The Spirit of the Lord [is] upon me, because he hath anointed me to preach the gospel to the poor; he hath sent me to heal the brokenhearted, to preach deliverance to the captives, and recovering of sight to the blind, to set at liberty them that are bruised."

-Luke 4:18

I went from *being a patient* in the waiting room to *being patient* in the waiting room.

God knows exactly what you need, my SUPER SINGLE sister. Wait on Him!

Set to Simmer

By Quiana, *Coupled*

I sit here as a 29-year-old woman, reflecting back on the past five years of my life— the moment of stillness and solace after a long-term relationship— and I don't regret them at all. A transition to a state of singleness was something that I had to get used to. Instead of wallowing in my time alone, I chose to take the time to do something that I'd never done: know myself. It sounds like such a cliché, but you really have to know who you are. I knew all of my bad habits, but I didn't quite know what made me tick or what my true motivations were.

I have built up a lot of confidence and happiness with my own self. Being able to reach happiness without someone else was an accomplishment for me as well as not having my emotions to be dependent on anyone else. All there was to worry about was me.

As I've gotten older, I realize that life is about living and experiencing things. It's funny how even though my mind is content with the single life, my heart still desires to feel the love it felt before, or a truer form of it. Perhaps what I thought was love at the time was something different. My heart still beats for the true definition. I still feel the strong pull of the tide.

Of course, I don't intend to rush out to sea. I like to take things slow because I think things set to simmer taste better. More flavorful. Everything has had a chance to mix well and sit right together. You've been through some heat, but you can always cool out to the right temp. I'm such a glutton for metaphors.

This time around, I'm taking 1 Corinthians 13:4-7 into account more often because it really is what it says:

4 Love is patient, love is kind. It does not envy, it does not boast, it is not proud. 5 It does not dishonor others, it is not self-seeking, it is not easily angered, it keeps no record of wrongs. 6 Love does not delight in evil, but rejoices with the truth. 7 It always protects, always trusts, always hopes, always perseveres.

I'm happy to say that I've found someone who truly encompasses that. Five years of simmering was worth it because what I have now came right on time. The perfect season and the right recipe.

Quiana is a freelance writer and graphic artist. She received a degree in graphic arts at Sessions Design School in New York. Her hobbies include digital photography and cooking. Her goal is to create a successful business in bath & body products.

The Right Focus

By Janee, *Free*

> *" Even youths grow tired and weary,*
> *and young men stumble and fall;*
> *but those who hope in the LORD*
> *will renew their strength.*
> *They will soar on wings like eagles;*
> *they will run and not grow weary,*
> *they will walk and not be faint."*

-Isaiah 40:30-31

Growing up, I was different. I began as a foster child. I was molested at the age of two by my foster mom's boyfriend. Being molested at such a young age caused major emotional and mental health problems. By the time I was four, I could not express myself in a healthy manner. I began to have preconceived notions about myself at my tender age. I hated myself. I felt ugly and worthless. Not to mention, I was the only one in my family who had a darker complexion. Because of this, I felt unwanted. Soon, I would realize that God was always with me.

God has always had a presence in my life. For instance, when I was four, I attended school at St. Thomas the Apostle Catholic School. There, the students attended mass weekly and on certain holidays, such as Christmas and Easter. While attending, I learned about suffering and how God is always with us, even in our darkest times.

Although I lived in abusive foster homes, I attended church faithfully. I also learned how to pray, but by the time I had gotten to middle school, my mind was constantly on boys and sex. To make matters worse, when I was eleven, I found out about masturbation! Because of this, I naturally wanted a boyfriend for the wrong reasons.

I had begun to go through various changes. I switched foster homes and schools twice in one year and was teased because I had the body of a grown woman. Boys my age wanted to hook up with me for that reason. This made me feel worse. When I reached high school, my reasons for having a boyfriend were so wrong that I was willing to do anything to get one.

As I reflect on high school, I have to say that I was not ok. I was emotionally unstable, mentally confused, and spiritually broken. Despite my problems, I still wanted to be in a relationship. During the summer of my senior year, I got my first boyfriend. I met him over the phone through a friend and didn't really care. I just wanted a boyfriend. Things started off good until I lost my virginity to him. Then he became controlling and hurtful. I came to my senses after three months and broke it off with him. Although our relationship didn't go well, I still yearned to have a boyfriend. After having been taken advantage of by two guys at the same time, I had a twisted outlook on love.

The last encounter I had with trying to look for love occurred with a guy who attended the church that I had just joined. I believed in my heart that God had sent this young man to be my husband. I found out later that He still needed to do work on him. After getting hurt repeatedly, I finally humbled myself to hear from God. Through fasting and seeking the Heavenly Father, He showed me that I didn't need to be super fine to be loved, nor would I have to give sexual favors. My mate would love me because I am me.

I soon realized that God wanted only greatness from me. I also learned that by being single, I am able to get closer to Him so that He can make me into the woman He wants me to be for my future husband.

In closing, I would like to say that the Lord has each of our best interests at heart. Waiting and leaning on Him will save us from a lifetime of heartache and pain. Trusting in what we can't see is difficult, but trusting in Jesus Christ...well that's what is best.

Janee is currently looking forward to beginning a career as a professional dancer. She formally attended Clark Atlanta University, but is now a graduate from Kaplan College for medical assisting.

I Am Healed

By Miss Flo, *Coupled*

> *"And we know that in all things God works for the
> good of those who love him, who have been called
> according to his purpose. For those God foreknew he
> also predestined to be conformed to the image of his
> Son, that he might be the firstborn among many
> brothers and sisters. And those he predestined, he also
> called; those he called, he also justified; those he
> justified, he also glorified."*
>
> *-Romans 8:28-30*

My name is Miss Flo and this is my story.

In 2006, a few months after graduating from Clark Atlanta University with a bachelor's in theatre arts, I started going with Bob (that's what we will call him). Bob was someone that I knew from a few summers of my childhood. He was staying with his grandmother at the time. His grandmother lives three houses away from my mom's house. It had been 11 years since we'd seen one another. Nevertheless, he came to my house to see me and we became a couple within two weeks. At the time, Bob, 25, was working as an electrician and had a son. Of course, he was the buff football player look that I'd always loved. Not to mention, he had dimples! I was more focused on who he was than his looks, but I have to be honest about his looks, ladies. I fasted and prayed for confirmation about this man. I had three dreams from the Lord, warning me about him, but I thought the dreams were inaccurate, since everything between us seemed so perfect.

We were together for a year and three months. Throughout the relationship, we had true ups and downs. I was being torn down more than what I could have ever realized. We only went on 2 or 3 dates out of the entire relationship and I paid at least two of those times! We went to his family's house a lot, which was fun, but he only used his money for himself. He was always asking me for money. He always hollered "broke" when he claimed to have been always working overtime, late hours, or many days in a row.

I had no peace when going out with friends. My phone was constantly being blown up (repetitive calling) and at the end of the night, my dad or friends would witness me being in a loud argument. I ended up crying and stressing over him, but by the end of the night--we were still a couple. We had many 10-minute breakups that resulted in tears and me feeling bad. Despite it all, I was sure that I had a good man because he was a hard worker and spent time with his son.

However, I will never forget the time that I followed him to his mother's house. He was driving his cousin's car and I was driving my car. While we were on the road, he called my cell. When I picked up, he repeatedly told me how "stupid, stupid, stupid" it was for me to drink. (Before we hit the road, I told him that I was a bit tipsy when I had gone to the club

the night before. I am delivered from drinking now.)
I asked my boyfriend to please stop using the word,
stupid, and not to talk to me that way. He refused to
stop and continued. When I called him stupid back it
was as if the enemy or a wild bear burst out of him!

I hung up the phone and turned around to
head home. He turned around to follow me and
called my cell over-and-over again. After not picking
up a few times, I finally answered the phone. I told
him that I was going home. He argued and told me I
was not and said that I was going to his mother's
house. When I asked why, he snapped, "Because I told
her you're coming, so you're coming." He kept
demanding that I go and was still following me back
home! After being pressured long enough, I turned
around and drove to his mother's house. We made up
after a talk with my friends and his step-dad who
shamed him for his behavior.

In our relationship, he tried to persuade my
friends that he was such a good man and that I was
giving him so many problems. At the end of our
relationship, they saw the truth.

The big thing in that relationship?? I
contracted genital herpes from this man. I was
manipulated into thinking that he did not cheat at all
and that he had no idea where it came from. *Yes, I
believed it!* I also stayed because I thought, *Well, hey,
we both got it now!* Three months later, I had to end
the relationship since his attitude had become
horrible toward me and my friends. We rarely saw
one another and my intuition (the Holy Spirit) was
telling me to get out before I entered a danger zone.

A week after the relationship ended, he was in a car with a girl in front of his house! Keep in mind that we stayed three houses away. Months after the relationship ended, God revealed to me that he was cheating! That was the most I had ever been hurt in my life. A few months after God revealed that, He also revealed to me through a neighborhood friend that Bob had more than one child. I found out that he was abusive, has had a restraining order, shacked up with women, and cheated on them like nobody's business! I had to give God the praise for His protection!

I prayed and spoke life and healing over my body. On October 31, 2008, one year and three months after the relationship, I received mail from Kaiser Permanente informing me that my Cervical test was normal, blood tests were negative, and that that there was no infection in my body. Hallelujah! I knew that God was a healer!

Since then, I have a new car, new home, new jobs and I feel great. I also met my prince charming that is ten times better than what I had before. As for Bob, he has another child, more drama, can't keep a job, and hasn't been stable in a woman's home.

Ladies, there is sunshine after the storm and life more abundantly. Giants fall! Don't let heartbreak be a stronghold because Jesus is the Lover of Our Soul.

God Bless,
Miss Flo

Miss Flo has recently completed her studies in the MA program of special education at Clark Atlanta University. Her bachelor's degree in theatre arts is also from CAU. She serves in dance ministry and in the Global Focus Group at Total Grace Christian Center. Miss Flo is also the president and overseer of FLONEA, which is a new ministry that began in 2010.

Idol Love: Self-Idolatry

By Gwendolyn M., *Free*

"Jesus said unto him, Thou shalt love the Lord thy God with all thy heart, and with all thy soul, and with all thy mind. This is the first and great commandment. And the second is like unto it, Thou shalt love thy neighbour as thyself. On these two commandments hang all the law and the prophets."

- Matthew 22:37-40

> *"I am the Lord your God, who brought you out of the land of Egypt, out of the house of bondage. You shall have no other gods before Me." -Exodus 20:2 (KJV)*

> *"4 You shall not make for yourself a carved image, or any likeness of anything that is in heaven above, or that is in the earth beneath, or that is in the water under the earth; 5 you shall not bow down to them nor serve them. For I, the Lord your God, am a jealous God, visiting the iniquity of the fathers on the children to the third and fourth generations of those who hate Me; 6 but showing mercy to thousands, to those who love Me and keep My Commandments." -Exodus 20:4-6 (KJV)*

The question has been posed over-and-over again by hurting women, "Why do I keep getting hurt?" The answer lies somewhere between "emotional reactivity" and sin. Our dominant quandary is the determination to find a lover, companion, husband, and friend. We have allowed emotional reactivity to define our intense, relentless search for love. It is this obsession with love that is idolatrous and all-consuming. It leaves no room for Christ's love in our hearts, souls, minds, and bodies. We are spiritually void of true love of which Christ is the foundation. The creature forsakes the Creator in order to satisfy the fleshy and seductive fires of desire.

I love to love. I am addicted to the feeling of love. I am a romantic lover. I am driven by romanticism. It has been a need that held me captive to self-indulgence, selfishness, self-focus, self-gratification, self-centeredness, self-absorption, self-abuse, self-determination, and self-satisfaction. I am accustomed to having my way. But love, well, I guess you could say it possessed me. I am someone who is impractical when it comes to love and loving. Love is an ideology and my ideas are based too much on my imagined idea of worldly, fleshly love.

I! I! I! At the center of sIn is "I," right? At the beginning of Idolatry is "I," right? Ladies, we can be our own worst downfall, not him.

I am writing to women of all ages, ethnicities, nationalities, race, creed, color, and those that are just like me. I am a fifty-something-year-old woman who, until recently, did not understand the root cause of my self-inflicted pain. My past pain does not define me and I am destined to repeat it until I pinpoint where it is coming from: It is coming from inside of me.

I am a hopeless romantic. No, let me correct that statement. I *was* a hopeless romantic. I can romance a cold-hearted man and fool myself into believing that the feeling is mutual. I have a sinful disease and other women have it, too. It is "idol love." The "wanting" of love becomes the driving force behind the search for love. When the wanting of love becomes impossible to differentiate from love itself, it is idol love. It is self-idolatry. It is a sin against God. It is a relationship doomed to fail from start to finish.

I was living for the day when someone would love me like I wanted and needed to be loved. This "self god" of mine led to a spiritual death. I loved. I begged for loved. I grieved for love and I have died a thousand deaths, it seems. The wages of sin is death. Idolatry leads to self-destruction and pain and anguish.

The Encarta English Dictionary defines an "idol" as (1) *object of adoration – somebody or something greatly admired or loved, often to excess; (2) object worshipped as god – something that is worshipped as a god, e.g. a statute or carved image; (3) forbidden object of worship – in monotheistic religions, an object of worship other than the one God.*

I was in love with the idea of being in love. I was in pursuit of love, the "feeling of being loved" since I was probably eight years old. It is a need that I have let overshadow my commitment as a Christian to love God more than anyone, even myself. He is a jealous God and the Lover of my Soul. I have been guilty of desecrating His temple (I belong to Him) with sexual immorality and sexual sin in an attempt to satisfy this craving. This lust of the flesh became for me— and some women like me— a graven image or, an idol god.

The Bible teaches us in Matthew 6:33, "But seek ye first the kingdom of God, and his righteousness; and all these things shall be added unto you." When Boaz found Ruth, she was being about her Father's business. She was not out searching for him. He [Boaz] was in search of her. She had her priorities straight. Put God first! Love God first and foremost and love will find us. *Love will find us!*

I realize at fifty-something the error of my ways in my quest to acquire and hold the "object" of my love captive. It is the "feeling" and the "wanting" that I was addicted to. I got up with it and I laid down with it at night. Romantic love is like an addiction. Some are addicted to drugs. Some are addicted to alcohol. Some are addicted to food. Some are addicted to sex. Some are addicted to pornography. Some are addicted to gossip. Some are addicted to pain. Some are addicted to thrill-seeking. Some are addicted to shopping and spending money. Some are addicted to idolatry. That would be me. I had an idolatrous addiction to "wanting" to be loved.

What was so unbelievable is that I did not know it, but Satan does. He knows our weaknesses and he is deceptively cunning in the traps he lays for us that can lead us away from God and straight to Hell. So ladies, listen with your heart, mind, and soul as I have revealed to you what the Holy Spirit has brought to light. My life is no longer defined by the pain I suffer when I am enslaved to an idol love god.

Now you know. Now you, too, can be set free and positioned for true love born of God. As for me, I turned from the idol god of selfishness to the One and true God of love, mercy, and grace. I know that if I love Him first with all of my heart, soul, and mind, love will find its way to me! It will find its way to you, too.

Gwendolyn is the eldest of six siblings. She has been ministering to others in song, since the age of eight, when she received her salvation and accepted Christ as her Lord and Savior. Her favorite hymn is "God's Amazing Grace," which was her mother's favorite hymn of praise and thanksgiving. Being a mother is her greatest success and the legacy she leaves the world is with her son and daughter. "They will do greater works in His name," is her prayer for them.

The Building Experience

By Carmen, *Coupled*

My name is Carmen and I am a graduate of Clark Atlanta University with a degree in public relations. I have been in a beautiful, challenge-filled, and growing relationship for the last four years.

Over the past four years, we have experienced some of the greatest joys and hardships. For the last two years, it has been a financial struggle that affected us both mentally and spiritually. This struggle led to sickness, frustration and unnecessary arguments, depleting happiness. But as we enter into our fifth year of being together, we now walk together in confidence and joy.

As we continue to grow in our relationship, we remember to love one another unconditionally and to the best of our abilities. If the love is real, one should be able to love the other at their best, worst, and in-between. At one point in our relationship, I saw him floundering in his life and regrettably thought about leaving him. I chose to stay because I realized that it was a moment of fear and not of God. A few months later, we found ourselves in the longest and hardest challenge we ever had to face. However, because we loved one another so much, our relationship became stronger than ever. We yelled and cried, but we also laughed, prayed, and enriched our strengths that were bestowed by God.

I must add that one should not suffer unnecessarily. Do not take all hardships as a sign of building a successful relationship. If the season is too rough and nothing gets better (the situation, the love, the bond, the spirit, or finances), then it is time to cut the rope and build a bridge into the future. Since we all face challenges, sometimes we have to pick what is worth fighting for and what is not.

Ladies, here are a few no-no's:
- fighting every day about the same thing, you will be miserable and never move forward
- Picking a fight with your significant other just because *you* have an issue
- Fighting about every-minute things (silly habits, routines, etc.)

The devil's tongue is wicked and slick and can work through you or others to jeopardize your blessing. Fortunately, I have not experienced the overly petty fights in this relationship. However, I have lashed out and caused an argument for my own insecurities or issues.

When your companion is a true "non-churchin" Christian, they know something so powerful that just may save your life: forgiveness. Here are some reasons for battles: selfishness, infidelity, withheld anger, distrust, lack of spirituality, abuse, laziness, and untrustworthy actions with finances. Understand what is meaningful enough to fight for and do not waste time or energy on something that will not matter in the next minute, hour, or day.

When it comes to spirituality with your companion, do not be afraid to share it. If the man is for you, it is imperative to understand your relationship with God and theirs. If they are lacking in their faith or vice-versa, that may not always be a sign to run. Take it as a growing experience and grow with your significant other. Your relationship with God must be strong enough to withstand what the world may bring to you.

While in the midst of our financial troubles, I began to lose faith. God sent me this man to keep my head up in praying for and with me to get stronger. I am blessed with true love. I love God and love the man that loves God.

There is indeed a time for everything under heaven as it says in Ecclesiastes 3:1-8. There is a time to plant your seed for a new life and a time to uproot it. There is a time for love and war and a time for hate and peace. In order to continue building yourself and your companion, follow the theory that was shared with me by my best friend and lover, Rashad. "Life is hard. Live harder. Love is hard. Love harder." And that, ladies, is God's honest truth!

Carmen Fletcher is an aspiring author with a focus on children's and young adult fiction. She has been in a committed relationship for five years and basks in the excitement and joy of the love she shares with her significant other. Her interests include writing, traveling, studying world culture education, and cooking. She is currently a bridal stylist for an international bridal brand. She looks forward to her future as a wife, mother, writer, and adventurer.

No Wonder Why I Was Wrong

By Marva, *Coupled*

"The heart is deceitful above all things and beyond cure; who can understand it?"

-Jeremiah 17:9

I often found myself losing faith in love, wondering if it was actually right for me. It seemed that everyone around me always got what they wanted, while all I ever did was want. I found myself getting frustrated and questioned why I even bothered having the desire to be in a relationship. As a single Christian woman, I looked for guys who could potentially be my husband. However, I found it pointless to try and find my potential mate in college. Most of the guys I talked to did not seem to value monogamy and/or upholding Christian values.

Most of them did not want to be in a relationship while in school. They felt that they would not be able to enjoy college if they were in a relationship. When I asked others why I didn't get the guy I wanted, all I heard was, "You have to go after what you want." I was taught that a man should pursue the woman and not the other way around, so I knew chasing a guy was out of the question. As a virgin at 21, I could not imagine what marriage would be like because it seemed as if guys my age did not uphold it as sacred. It seemed as if they couldn't see the forest for the trees. I even wondered, *Is it worth waiting? Will I regret waiting?*

Being faced with this conundrum, however, led me to receive a word from the Holy Spirit. I realized that my mindset was all wrong. I was wrong for putting my faith in love and not in the one who gives *unconditional* love. I was wrong for believing that my virginity was not valued. I was wrong for allowing my desire for love to almost cause me to leave my heart in the wrong hands. I was wrong, most of all, for not trusting God. The Bible teaches, "Man looks at the outward appearance, but God looks at the heart" (1 Samuel 16:7). Remembering this now relieves my frustration from when guys told me I am "wifey material," but never fathomed having a relationship with me. Knowing that I am loved by my Father and knowing that my heart is in his hands for safe keeping, has helped me to enjoy being single.

Failed attempts to typecast the guy that I thought was best for me helped me to realize that I needed to let God choose my mate. I know now that God knew my needs, even when I thought that I knew them. The reason why things have worked out the way they have in my life is because God knows my heart and He knows who is right for me. I needed to let the Holy Spirit be my spiritual x-ray to see my potential mate for who he really is.

God is our strength and our guiding light. We should not judge someone based on what we think we know about them. We should instead ask God to judge who has our best interest at heart and who does not. I have learned that it is important to step aside and allow God more space to help us make informed decisions. I was reminded that I have to protect my body because many people try to get in and destroy it. God will supply our needs, so if we ask him, He will answer. I was wrong for not valuing what God deemed so precious. I was being too impulsive to find someone. I no longer wonder because my Daddy knows best. No wonder why I was wrong!!

Marva is a graduate of Claflin University with a bachelor's degree in English. She enjoys meeting people, spending time with God, reading, writing and skating.

The Best Dress

By Adelia, *Free*

How do you pick your dresses?

Oooh, there it is! The perfect one and it looks my size. My color. It accents every part of me that makes me sexy. Then when you get it on, it doesn't quite, ummm, fit? Maybe it's a bit too tight. A bit too revealing? Not classy enough? Now that your perception of perfect is misconstrued, you have two options: buy the dress and make it fit, or walk away and know that there may be something better waiting. Option Two will require much more patience and much more understanding of yourself. This may take a while. Now, if we all picked our men the way we picked our dresses, how much more comfortable would we be in our own skin?

Option One may leave you feeling insecure and not so sure if people will stare because that dress is complimenting your true beautiful essence...or is it distorting what God has naturally given you? You may slip on an undergarment to smooth away the things that you don't want people to see, but what do you do when you get home and the distorted, perfect dress is off? You are still stuck with the same insecurities from when you left. You are no longer shielded by the help of an illusion. Ladies, the dress that you take your time to purchase should have you feeling confident about yourself. It should have you feeling bold. When you walk the roads, people will look at you in awe, wanting to go buy the same dress. We are not all meant to wear the same dress, so be comfortable with yours and know that it doesn't fit on anyone else, but you.

From personal experience, I know that it becomes stressful and annoying to try on different dresses. However, when you do find the one that fits, you'll know it. At this point, ladies, I hope that I have given you a metaphor in which you can relate. Dating men can be very complicated and to compare the matter to dresses definitely simplified it for me. Some may think it's not that easy, but what we must understand is that we serve a God that does things in decency and in order (1 Corinthians 14:40). According to God, it can be this simple. Perhaps humans are the ones that make things complicated.

In addition to having the "dress" that fits you, you have to have the necessary accessories to go along with it. You want accessories that will bring out the beauty of that dress and compliments *you*. Having a good man is great, but what about the accessories? How does he treat strangers? How does he respond to someone in need? How does he respond to you when you are having a bad day? How spiritually in-tuned is he? These are necessary accessories that should coincide with who he is. Some appear to be the perfect dress, but when you put on the accessories, you see that it doesn't quite compliment you like you thought it would, which is why 2 Corinthians 6:14 is so important. It mentions that we are not to be yoked with unbelievers. We should not link ourselves to someone or something, dresses or men, that will deter us from serving God.

Be encouraged. Once you get on track with God's plan, you will not experience heartbreak. Impossible, you say? Well, you have ultimate control of your emotions and if a man won't love you the way you want to be loved, God will. If a man doesn't care enough to fulfill your heart's desires, God will. If a man wants to leave you for another woman, let him go. See it as a sign that God has something bigger and better for you. The only way to really know a life free of worries is to know and trust God. Remind yourself of the spiritual goodness that God has bestowed upon you. When you get your dress, flaunt it. Remind him daily how good God is. You want a man to love you the way he loves God and himself.

Adelia is from Atlanta, GA. She attended school at Clark Atlanta University. She is currently working on becoming a teacher and hopes to open her own school.

Looking Back,
but Looking Forward

By Amanda, *Free*

*"In all thy ways acknowledge him and he shall direct
thy paths."*

–Proverbs 3:6

I have always loved *love* and the thought of
being in love. When I see couples, it genuinely warms
my heart and makes me smile. Coming up, I didn't
have many boyfriends or people that liked me (that I
knew of). My father was in my life, but he wasn't *in*
my life, so I found myself longing for love from the
opposite sex.

In high school, guys would always look, but
would never say anything to me. I dreamed of having
a high school sweetheart to spend the rest of my life
with, but once I stepped into the doors of Mays High I
knew that there was a slim chance of finding Mr.
Right.

Everyone always talks about how when you
are young you should keep your options open and
not be tied down, but I wanted that one person to be
with to share all of my sorrows, insecurities and
happiness. For a while, I thought that I had found
him. I prayed for a great guy and God sent him to me.
He was there for me in every way possible. He went

out of his way to make up for the things that I did not get growing up. If there was ever a moment where I felt down about something or was stressed out, he was there to lift me up with his jokes and kind words. When there were problems at home and I just needed to get away, I could count on him to pick me up and take me away like Calgon.

I can say that if I never experience love again, I loved that man with every inch of my being. Because of my lack of experience in relationships and personal insecurities, I lashed out a lot. I did not like to be wrong or admit that I was wrong about anything. About 2 years into our relationship, things got really rocky and I did not understand why. I begged and pleaded with God to keep him in my life, even when things had gotten really bad between us. I asked God to reveal to me if he was supposed to be in my life because it had become a physical, mental, and emotional strain on both of us. Instead of just moving on, we both were trying to hold on. No matter how many signs were thrown in my face from God, I would always find a way around them. We would continue to break up and later, make up.

Proverbs 16: 9 reads, "A man's heart plans his way, but the Lord directs his steps."

I ran across this scripture while writing this and it touched me so much. It took me back to all the times that I tried to be the lead and when I focused in, God was always ahead of me.

Almost a year after we broke up, I finally began to let go.

I do not know what my future holds with finding love. I can only ask God to send me who He has for me, if there is someone, and I must wait patiently. It is tough because my heart still aches from my first real relationship. I have suffered serious blows to my self-esteem in recent years, so it is hard to trust anything that guys say about me or to me. This makes it extremely hard to date. All I can do is trust in God. I know that He will provide and make me a happy woman someday.

Amanda holds a bachelor's degree in business administration from Georgia State University. She is an aspiring model and has done numerous runway shows. She aspires to build a portfolio in the coming years. She plans to own her own clothing boutique in the near future, as well.

A Love Story

By Barbara, *Free*

"For I reckon that the sufferings of this present time are not worthy to be compared with the glory which shall be revealed in us."

- Roman 8:18

He loved me and that was all that mattered. The ambivalence from my mother, the warnings from my friends, and even his family did not matter. He loved me. Wasn't that enough?

To appreciate this, you must first realize that I was that girl who had her first child at the age of 13 in a town of only 13,000 or so. Forrest City, AR, to be precise. I was the girl who the popular kids would speak to only because I was smart, but their parents wouldn't allow them to hang with me. The girl who did not have her own boyfriend because, "Who wants a ready-made family?" But everybody's man from hers-to-yours flirted with me on the low because, "If she got a baby she must be...."

So when he came along, all fine and muscular and red-boned in his big ol' truck and running behind *me,* I fell in love. Drugs, sex, and the notoriety of being his woman sent me to levels I had never been before. Mama said not to marry him, but I was rebellious. With my headscarf on and he in his shorts, we stood in front of his grandfather and got married. It was beautiful. My man was as tough as nails and he actually cried! My cousin drove his truck around town that night, while we lay in bed on the back of it under the stars. Romantic, right? Not so much.

When he told me that people asked why he was with "ugly old me," I believed him. When he used to put hot spoons on areas I can't mention, it must have been because I was in the wrong. And when he choked me until I passed out, and later breathed into my mouth, I looked at him as a savior.

Foolish, huh? But all the while, something was growing on the inside of me. A voice saying, *"Go! Run! You are Sharon's daughter, Bertha's niece, Carey's child, Flotille's granddaughter! Go! Run!"*

He went to jail, so I hit the club and enjoyed a whim of freedom. It was there that a young man told me, "You look good, but the trouble your man will bring ain't worth me talking to you, 'cause your man is crazy." *Wait, didn't my man say people thought I was ugly?*

He came home.

It was okay for a day or so, until we went to Sunrise, his neighborhood where everyone knew and/or feared him. He said that I was flirting with his boy, but it was all in his mind. My eyes were for him alone. After all, I had long ago learned not to even look at another guy from fear of his reaction.

Later, the man that I loved drove me to the lake and told me to swim or he'd shoot me! I grew guts that day because I was more afraid of the water than him. "Shoot me then!" I yelled. Strangely enough, he took me home!

It is funny now because that water probably only reached my knees. That night, I put my babies in his big red truck and drove to Jonesboro, while he slept. No it wasn't an easy journey...but well worth it.

I thank God for my experience with that man. It sent me on a journey, not only for my salvation, but to my *salvation*. Had I not left my husband, I may have never left and moved to Jonesboro, AR and then to Little Rock, where I met my pastor and his wife. Now, here is my story. I am a youth director, church member, college student, and proud mama! I pray only the best for that man. I pray that God raises him up and uses him that He may receive the glory out of his life!

Just as the scripture says, the suffering of those former times is nothing compared to the glory that God is getting out of my life!

Ms. Celie said, "I may be black, I may be ugly, but I'm here!"

Ms. Barbara says, "I am black, I know I'm beautiful, and look where God has brought me!"

Barbara is a Christian, single mother who works in the education field and is the Youth Director at Victorious Living Ministries in Little Rock, Arkansas. She has a passion for encouraging and reaching out to at-risk girls. Barbara is also an avid reader and writer.

I Would Be His Ruth,
He Would Be My Boaz

By Duanne, *Engaged*

October 1, 2006—

The sun was shining bright, my afro was glistening, my veil was blowing in the wind, and there wasn't a hint of sweat on my full white dress! What a glorious occasion for two to become one before God! We'd approached the portion of the ceremony when we were to gaze into each other's eyes and say our vows.

"For richer or richer..."

After the words flowed from my mouth, I remember hearing the laughter and thinking, *I'm so serious!* "For richer or for poorer" just didn't seem right. *How can you ever be poor when your life is full of love and blessings from our Lord and Savior Jesus Christ?* The ceremony was beautiful and the reception just as fabulous. I couldn't wait to pick up my life and move from Georgia to California with my new husband.

Just eight months shy of marriage, the man that promised God and me, "I do," decided that life was too much for him to handle. He disappeared for three days and on the fourth day, I received a visit from the county's coroner telling me that he'd taken his own life.

I was devastated, lost, confused, and hurt. I could list numerous adjectives. After blurred moments of weakness and despair, I remembered my favorite bible verse: Romans 8:28 which says, "And we know that all things work together for good, to those who love God, to those who are the called according to His purpose."

All things work together! All things! How amazing and mind-boggling is that? All things aren't good, nor do all things work together for good for all people all the time. I was devastated, but faithful and prayerful that He would work things out for me. All I had to do was answer His call.

Six months later, a man whom I'd never met, but had been life-long friends with his family, asked for my business card. We were both at a baby shower for his cousin where I happened to be the pastry culinarian for the event. I didn't give him my card, but I added him to my email list. At the time I didn't know that this man would be my guardian angel, my prayer partner, my confidant, and my future husband. I would be his Ruth and he would be my Boaz.

Do you know the story of Ruth? Ruth was a widow, and so was her mother-in-law, Naomi. During the biblical times, when a woman's husband died, a young widow was expected to return to her family, her people. However, Ruth made a pledge to stay with her mother-in-law. While dwelling with Naomi, Ruth stayed faithful and prayerful to God that all things would work together for good in her life. She eventually won the respect and love of Boaz, who was a rich and influential man who lived in Bethlehem.

God will use your faithfulness to accomplish His extraordinary plans. I knew that God had a Boaz waiting for me and I claimed it! Now that I have him, I can't imagine anyone more extraordinary than he. His laugh, his smile, his touch, his love for me, brings out the sun during the worst thunderstorm. Oh, how amazing God is for sending him to me to end the storm in my life! I can't wait to commit and submit my life to him in the same way Ruth did to Naomi in Ruth 1:16-17,

"But Ruth said:
'Entreat me not to leave you,
Or to turn back from following after you;
For wherever you go; I will go;
And wherever you lodge, I will lodge;
Your people shall be my people,
And your God, my God.
Where you die, I will die,
And there will I be buried.
The Lord do so to me, and more also,
If anything but death parts you and me.'"

Remain faithful in God's faithfulness. Read His word daily. Thank Him daily for all the blessings that have overflowed and the abundance of blessings to come. Pray for a listening ear that you may answer His call, so that He may work things out for the good in your life.

Duanne is a graduate of Fort Valley State University. She currently works for a FORTUNE 1000 company and owns and operates Edible Praise, LLC, a personal chef service. She enjoys traveling, volunteering with AFSP initiatives and spending time with friends and family.

Love, Labeled

By Raine, *Free*

"Love never fails..."

- 1 Corinthians 13:8

We were going to get married and I thought that we had overcome the heartache. After loving someone for so long, I have come to learn that it doesn't mean that they will love you the same in return. Sometimes when they do start to truly love you, it's too late. The love you had is gone and you don't want to give it away anymore.

My first love and I had a good, long, 2 years of no fighting, cheating, or lies. We used to do a lot together, such as walking to the park, and having picnics with one hoagie, chips, and a 2-liter soda. I remember one time he saved a bird for me that was stuck in the mud. He was really showing me that he loved me. To me, it was cute, and it made me happy. For a while, everything seemed as if nothing could go wrong and I was in love so deep that I had become blind.

That blind love is what my dad calls it.

My dad explained to me the many labels that he has for love: Stupid love, puppy love, hate love, lust love, you name it, my dad said it.

Now, I was so happy and in love that I didn't even notice when the lies and cheating had started. I started to notice that he was changing on me again and nothing that I did mattered. *I want to save our relationship! We have a child together and I am in love with you!* I thought.

I remember when I first found out that he was cheating with this girl. At the time, I was 8 months pregnant. I went out for a while with my mother and came back home to an empty room. His clothes were gone, as well as his shoes, coat, and colognes. I started to panic and ran to his mother and asked, "Where is my beloved, mom?" She looked at me and with a voice that I had never heard before replied," Baby, he's left you."

I felt my heart jump out of my chest! I wanted to die right then and there! I packed my things and moved out of his mother's house. Maybe 2 weeks went by and he returned with his soothing words, "Renee I love you!"

"Renee you know I didn't mean it,"

"You know where my heart is."

Just like my dad had explained, there are many names for love and I had stepped on the stupid side of it because I took him back. I loved him and in my heart knew that he wanted to do better. I knew that he loved me like I loved him.

Finally, the time came when he wanted us to get married. I said yes. He later got locked up and I didn't even care. I was so in love that I was setting everything up for us to get married in the prison. I was going to make this family work! I was dead-set on us being one, being a family and having a father for my son.

I wasn't thinking. A month before we were to get married, he called me and said that he had to confess something. I remember my reply to him like it was yesterday: "Beloved, nothing you can tell me will stop me from loving you."

He answered, "I had sex with your sister at my mom's house while you were sleep in the bed."

I remember my breathing becoming harder and harder as if I couldn't get any air. I felt my whole world falling. I could only do one thing and that was to hang up. I was so hurt that I had become a drinker. Also, I hated my sister for a long time and him as well. I soon trusted no one, I started to drink so much that it clouded my thinking.

I even premeditated how I was going to pay him back for destroying my life. In the end, however, I only hurt myself. I started to play the tick for tack game. The payback game. It lasted for at least 6 months until my best friend woke me up. She loved me so much that she told me exactly how I was looking and exactly how she was feeling. A smack to the face and her screaming and crying at me woke me up. I am thankful for my best friend to this day!

At the end of this ordeal, I learned that no matter how hard you love someone it does not mean that they will love you back the same way. You can continue to love them until it hurts or sometimes kills. I can't love anymore like I once did because I am scared of the outcome, so I keep my distance. Even my sister and I have not had a good relationship since this happened. Although they both hurt me, I still help them when I can because I do love them—but from a distance. A distance so far that they won't ever know how much I love them. Or maybe they do because they can feel it and see how much they both hurt me.

As I share this story, I hope that we will never give our all if we are not getting our lover's all in return. My motto is: "Fairly take and fairly give in a relationship." In the beginning of a relationship, we should talk and learn about the other person in order to know what we're getting into before we get into it.

My sisters, what you go through in life can sometimes turn you into a cold-hearted woman who will never receive love because you are unsure if you want it again. Guard your heart! Take time to heal for all the times you did not. When love comes knocking again, remember my dad's names for it and choose your relationship wisely! Love with your eyes open, so you both can see the clouds and stay grounded!

One love.

Raine was born in Trenton N.J., in December on a beautiful winter day. She is now a mother of five wonderful children that she breathes for everyday. She has learned that in life, if she can help at least one person, she is doing some good in the world. She fairly takes, fairly gives, and harms none.

Nukesha's Story

By Nukesha, *Free*

"But seek first his kingdom and his righteousness, and
all these things will be given to you as well."

-Matthew 6:33

Sometimes, *Once upon a time* never ends in, *happily ever after.*

At least that's how my love life seemed. I searched for love in all the wrong places, in men, friends, and material things. They all gave me something that I never truly desired— temporary thrills. I often felt that if I pleased everyone else, gave them my all, I could get that and more in return. Little did I know, I had it calculated all wrong. In relationships, I was taught that what I wouldn't do, the next woman would. Whatever it takes to please and make my man happy, I must do. I quickly learned that a man was going to do what he wants no matter what I did. I thought, *Does he love me like I love him? Or, is this thing that I feel called lust?*

When it came to my friends, I was the one to stand by every syllable of that word. If that meant getting out of my bed at 3 a.m. or simply giving you my last two dollars, I did it. What did I get in return when I needed help? Nothing! I was left with the very short end of the stick many times. I was brokenhearted, shattered into millions of pieces, and much like Humpty Dumpty. No one could ever put this thing back together again. That was until I learned *whose* I am. I learned that I couldn't love anything or anyone until I loved myself.

At the tender age of eighteen, I met the love of my life, my best friend, and future husband— or so I thought. He had a way with words that left me speechless. He was a tall, dark, handsome pretty boy that didn't mind getting his hands dirty. He was every girl's dream and every woman's nightmare.

I sought him before I sought God. A sister was in love and I gave him more than all of me for almost a year. I remember sitting at the computer, checking emails, when I received a message from a much older woman. She wanted to know how I knew my current boyfriend and how long we had been dating. I was in shocked when I read, "He's been my boyfriend for years. We are in an open relationship and you are being played." This had to be a mix-up, wrong email account, or something. I immediately confronted him. He didn't deny nor acknowledge what I had come to know was, in fact, true. He simply said, "She's crazy. Don't even bother responding to her."

Things ended and I was one emotional wreck. I depended on the emotional support of others and church sermons to recover. A year had passed and he was ready to try this again. Naïve, I agreed. Five years later, things still hadn't gotten any better. He was still playing the field, even with a marriage proposal. I made up in my mind that I had nothing left to fight for. *But how do I end this?*

One Sunday morning, I was sitting in church, heartbroken, and searching for answers to my questions. "Let go and let God," were the next words spoken out of my pastor's mouth. "While you are trying to figure it out, God has already worked it out." That was it! God was still there, although I had put him on the back burner. Things could have been prevented if only I had catered to Him more.

1 Corinthians 13:2-13 taught me what love really is, God loves me unconditionally and though the fairy tale with my ex didn't end with happily ever after, my first love (God) was always there to welcome me with open arms. If I knew then what I know now, I would have kept my focus on the Lord.

Nukesha resides in Little Rock, Arkansas. She is a graduate of John L. McClellan Business Magnet High and currently works as a home health aide. She enjoys writing poetry, reading books, bowling, and spending time with family.

Listen to Me:
Love Is a Blessing Business

By Desirable Queen, *Free*

"Now that you have purified yourselves by obeying the truth so that you have sincere love for your brothers, love one another deeply, from the heart."

- I Peter 1:22

No bliss.

It's a real trip going down this road we call relationships. He said, "My momma told me that you were my wife."

The Queen is like, "Do what? Ok, your mother don't know me from Adam. When did this come about?"

"She didn't just tell me. It's been some time ago. Look, I don't want to be a disappointment."

Too late. You are already headed down that road with your negativity. Oh, I get it. My frame ain't small enough for you? Baby, don't get it twisted. There's a 28-year-old who's texting or calling me everyday, wanting to put me on his throne.

I know things may be pleasing, polite, gentle, and trouble free for the time being, but your boat is beginning to rock. Slowly, but surely it is going into an uncontrollable spiral. Baby, know the worth of your relationship before you end up going on a guilt trip when my hand into another brother's hand slips because you, while living in a fantasy world, lost your grip. Maybe that was the problem.

You did grasp my attention. You held it for a while, but you didn't have control. It wasn't substantial. It wasn't real. It wasn't genuine. We have been in and out of each other's lives for over a decade.

You still got wild oats you need to sow? Baby, everything that glitters ain't gold.

I am a woman of refinement through a process that we call life. I don't need a man to buy me a house or a car. I got that covered, bro. What I need is a loving heart, the same as mine, to lavish this love upon.

Wake up. Open your eyes. I'm standing right in front of you. Queen is the name they've given me, unless with "woman of the night" is where you'd rather be. That woman's arrogance, vanity, conceit, greed will eventually cause you grievance. She loves what you can do for her, she doesn't love you. Truth be told, it's not even about you, but you couldn't see past those jeans she was wearing.

I know your momma told you that everything that looks good to you ain't good for you. You should have listened. Just know that through all of your bad days and tough times, I kept you uplifted in prayer. I asked God to keep your mind in perfect peace. That "woman of the night" turned her back on you and walked away. I don't want to be the Queen of someone else's throne, but I have got to right this wrong. My love for you will forever be infinity.

Desirable Queen is a single, 41-year-old mother of one. She hasn't had the pleasure of marital bliss, but believes that God is still in the blessing business. She believes also that she is too blessed to be living in distress. Desirable Queen is a customer service manager for a major retail chain. Spiritual, caring, charming, kind-hearted, lover of life are words best used to describe her personality. Her hobbies consist of making others happy, whether it is in a wedding, anniversary, birthday, baby shower, retirement party, or family reunion. She loves to plan and make those days the most memorable. It does her heart good to make others happy.

My Baali, My Ishi

By Gerria, *Divorced*

It was in my wilderness that God asked me to marry Him. I am not of the Catholic faith, so becoming a nun was not an option. Besides, after being celibate for two years already, I knew that the vow of a nun was not one that I was willing to take for a lifetime. What did God want from me then? And how could I become betrothed to the Creator of all things?

The revelation of God's call on my life began with a very simple, but profound scripture - Hosea 2:16 (NKJV). The scripture reads, " 'And it shall be, in that day,' says the Lord, 'That you will call Me 'My Husband (Ishi),' And no longer call Me 'My Master (Baali).'" The remarkable thing is that this call came to me in a time when I was arguably at the lowest point I had ever been in my life. I was still healing from a broken marriage and subsequent divorce; I was bankrupt, both financially and emotionally; I had only a few worldly possessions left. My daughter, 13 at the time, served as my only source of happiness.

Yet, here was God, whom I had accepted into my life as a child, in the person of Jesus Christ, asking me to reach through all of the darkness in my life and find Him in that darkness. I did not know where to start, so I prayed for help. It was in prayer that the awesomeness of God's request began to surround me and seep into my spirit. Almighty God wanted an intimate relationship with me! He was calling me closer and deeper into His will. He was ready to open my spiritual eyes to the wonder of His mysteries so that I could begin to know Him and not just about Him.

How mind-blowing it is that the perfect Creator would take notice of this broken, flawed, and wounded person, and with all my imperfections, bid me come closer to His throne?! At first, I was consumed by how unworthy I actually was (and still am) of such an honor. Yet, my Lord, my Baali, spoke His eternal love and mercy to my spirit every day, until my esteem and my confidence were restored through Him. Every bird sang for me; every breeze blew for me; the warmth of the sun was just for me. He had always seen my true worth even though I had let the clouds of my circumstances overshadow the gift of His light in my life.

Today, I am still learning to walk in intimacy with Christ, yet He remains patient, loving, and merciful through it all. His Spirit teaches me that I am Esther, having access to my King and all that He possesses. He whispers to me that I am Mary Magdalene, walking closely with Him and ministering to the needs of His kingdom. He speaks to my spirit that I am Mary, mother of Christ, whom He will use to birth forth precious seeds of truth, wisdom, and love. Yet, the sweet rapture of this intimacy is not just reserved for me.

Jesus stands waiting for all who will come to Him and in faith, will take a vow of marriage: "Yes, Lord, I will take you as my Ishi, to have for eternity and to hold dear to my heart, loving, honoring, and obeying you, through seasons of prosperity as well as seasons of sowing, until my human death returns my soul to you to dwell with you forever. Amen.

Gerria lives in the Atlanta metro area. She is the proud mom of a beautiful daughter. Gerria works in accounting and writes poetry and free verse in her free time.

Unexpectedly Super Single

By Gwendolyn J., *Widowed*

"Lead me in thy truth, and teach me: for thou art the God of my salvation; on thee do I wait all the day."

-Psalm 25:5

Stuff happened like a diagnosis of cancer. Eleven months to cram a bunch of living into a short amount of time and then, suddenly single for the first time in thirty-three years. That began in the year 2000, abruptly another way of existence that caught me totally unprepared to handle it. Me? I can handle anything. I am a good person, so why would this be my fate? Together for the rest of my life. Well, our lives, you know, sixty or seventy years.

But single I have become and single, I am.

Ten years in July. Wow! Who knew that it would be like this? In some ways, it is freedom the hard way and in other ways, I somewhat adjusted to life on my own. You see, I have only been single for about the last three or four years. Before that, I was married in mind and deed, not wanting a real relationship because that would be wrong. Sabotage was the master plan. Best not to let any man get too close. Therefore, I would wreck it before it became serious.

Believe me when I say that I had my hand in blocking them out, but my hand was not the only hand in the mix. The Lord has a plan and you can try to sidestep it if you want to, but ultimately, it will be His way. What is she talking about now? A riddle wrapped up in a mystery. I never quite say what I know to be the truth about my situation.

The truth is I like being by myself. There are no restrictions on my time. I can do whatever I want and the only one I have to answer to is God. That is the way He wants it for now. Sure, it would be nice to have companionship every now and then, but even that comes with a price that I am not willing to pay at this time in my life. Instead of focusing on getting a man, it is on my getting to know my God and sharing an intimacy unlike anything I have ever known.

Life with my late husband was wonderful, but I was a wife subject to him. Raising our children and grandchildren was an experience that I was blessed to have, but I was a mother responsible for helping to shape and mold them for their own life experiences. Now I am I, myself, and me. I am finally learning my purpose and how I fit in the big scheme of things called life.

I have tried my hand at dating and someone even proposed marriage, which I considered for awhile. Does having a man validate any woman as a worthwhile person? No, having a man will not make you happy or content if you are not content all by yourself. I have learned that happiness comes from within and we are responsible for maintaining it. I will not let people bring me down by making me feel incomplete because I have chosen to let the Lord orchestrate the next relationship. It is my choice to be whole all by myself than one-half with the wrong person.

There is a saying that I can do bad all by myself, but guess what? I am not doing badly at all. In fact, life is wonderful with so many up and downs, turns and twists, and tests and trials. The opportunities are limitless with freedom to take advantage of them.

In conclusion, but far from the end, I am living the life of Riley—whoever that is. Actually, I have surrendered my life to become a useful vessel, manipulated by the Potter's Hands to turn any way that He deems appropriate. As super singles, our position is perfect to be just what God wants us to be. It is not an accident or coincidence that at this moment—and a moment it may be—that we are alone. Destiny is in control and has to play out as set in time. He knows when to have Mr. Wonderful come to you and grin in your face. Give Him your life and He will put a better life in your giving.

In 1998, Gwendolyn J. helped to found the Abundant Harvest Church of God in Christ Buffalo, NY with her late husband. Ms. Jackson is in love with her Lord and Savior Jesus Christ and He is in love with her. Gwendolyn is happy to live a life of blissful service to the Lord. Her passion in writing lead to her becoming an author, songwriter, speaker, actor, and many other endeavors. She is the president of NCOURAGEME 2B UNLIMITED, a motivational consulting business which has helped develop her gift in order to bring out the gifts in others.

Something Good *Is* Coming Out of This, Right?

By Courtney A., *Free*

"'Wait on the Lord: be of good courage, and He shall strengthen thine heart: wait, I say, on the Lord.'"

-Psalm 27:14

The hardest word in this scripture is *wait*. To *wait* on something is to be in a state of expectation for something to happen. As Christians, we expect God to work all of our situations out in our favor. However, we quickly forget that there are things that we must do. Pray. Fast. Worship. These are all actions, so we must first have faith and trust God to complete these actions and eventually see change.

Waiting equals patience and patience is a virtue. In the process of waiting, you become a 'virtue-ous' (virtuous) woman. A true man of God prays for the virtuous woman found in Proverbs 31. A virtuous woman is full of goodness, love, faithfulness and kindness. If you look closely, these are actually the Fruits of the Spirit, which are love, joy, peace, patience, kindness, goodness, faithfulness, gentleness, and self-control. In order to have the

Fruits of the Spirit, you must *live* by the Spirit. In order to live by the Spirit, you must *know* the Spirit.

The only way that you can get to know the Spirit is by entering into a relationship with God. In the process of getting to know God, you also get to know yourself. After all, He is the one who created you and to love God is to love yourself. Your marriage should be a reflection of your relationship with God, which means that your husband must also be in a relationship with God. Marriage is not just a covenant between a man and woman, but also, with God.

"And we know that all things work together for good to them that love God, to them who are called according to His purpose" (Romans 8:28). If you develop a love for God from your relationship with Him, then what do you have to worry about? By loving God, you must have so much faith and trust in Him that you can wait. *Faith and trust. Aren't these two qualities that a man and woman must embody in order to have a healthy relationship?* I'm 24 and many of my friends always question why I don't date a lot of people. My response to them is that I must grow in God first because as a result of becoming one with Him, He will give me discernment to know when the right man will enter my presence.

Over the last few months, God has blessed me with many business ventures. Who's to say that I won't meet my husband at one of those business events? After all, Ruth didn't meet Boaz until she went out into the field. My husband is not supposed to complete me, but he must add to me and I to him. In order to recognize that a man is adding to me, I must know my value and worth and have my own life. Trust me ladies, I know that it does get hard sometimes. Then I begin to think, *Would I rather get married quickly to a man only to be divorced a few months later? Or should I wait on the man that God designed just for me and me for him? The man that I will minister to God's people and save souls with for eternity?*

If you do not remember anything else from this article, please reflect on this: God commands us to love our neighbors as we love ourselves. The most powerful part is "loving ourselves." So love yourself and wait on God to bless you with the good man who will know that he must love you more than he loves himself.

Courtney A. is a graduate of Spelman College. Born and raised in South Carolina, she currently resides in Marietta, GA, and is the CEO/Grants Manager of FAVOR Grant Consulting, which is a company that provides grant writing and business development services for non-profit organizations and individual business owners. She is also a background vocalist for Lynntesha Roberts & D'Vyne Faith and is working toward becoming an attorney.

Him, First

By Rebecca, *Free*

> *"Do not be anxious about anything, but in everything by prayer and petition, with thanksgiving, present your requests to God."*
>
> *-Philippians 4:6*

I do not care about your background and whether or not you have a great mom or dad. It does not matter. Even if you were abandoned or your parent(s) died, everybody plays a fool when it comes to relationships...sometimes. The only way to make it is to have God as a very strong foundation. Proverbs 3:5-6 reads, "Trust in the Lord with all your heart and lean not on your own understanding; in all your ways acknowledge him, and he will make your paths straight."

Even with God, you can still have problems because you didn't listen to his instructions or warnings about the relationship. Believe me, everybody receives a warning from God about future outcomes of a relationship, but we must take heed. Pray for a receiving heart that you will do whatever He asks of you.

One important thing is to always pray when you first start developing feelings. This can stop a lot of future heartbreak. Yeah there might not be anybody when the smoke clears, but you are waiting on "the one." One day he will still stand there when it is all said and done. The prayer that I say to God is, "Lord, bring it to something or bring it to nothing." It always works.

While you are waiting, the spirit of loneliness can set in, you must pray it away. If you are so anxious, you will get something you wished you would have never gotten involved with. You will wish that you had waited on the Lord. Pray, always pray. I cannot stress this enough.

There was a time that I didn't look at the whole picture when I thought about what I wanted in a man. Now I have a list of my realistic needs. Ladies, this is serious. You cannot write a list with a certain eye color, hair, skin texture, and body type as the only qualities required. You will only have a vain list of a superficial man. My list consists of most of my needs based on what I did not get in the last relationship. You can get a man to check off all of your qualities on the list, if you just wait and pray.

Exodus 20:3 reads, "You shall have no other gods before me."

I remember putting my love and obedience for God second. I traded my covenant with Him for the love of a man. I thought, *Wow! I have made this love searching into a god and anybody that would give it to me would be my god.* I had to change that because putting Jesus first is the only way to go. The other way leads to many tears.

Rebecca is a believer in Christ, prospective grad student, future entrepreneur, and developer of her God-given gifts. She is a lover of art, which includes everything that God created from the earth and all of its glory. She is a connoisseur of all music and cultures.

Love Hurts

By Tonya, *Free*

"Wherefore I say unto thee, Her sins, which are many, are forgiven; for she loved much:but to whom little is forgiven, [the same] loveth little."

-Luke 7:47

I thought that he was my first rebound in the beginning, but as time passed, I felt myself growing attached to this man. When I didn't hear from him, I found myself contemplating on what he was doing that kept him from reaching out to me. I thought, *We both missed work to spend a whole day together. Our bodies were just connected the night before, so why the distance? Who is with him?* So the more I thought about him being with another woman, the weaker I became. Oh, but when I heard from him, I disregarded the previous tears and missed meals. He rejuvenated me. He brought happiness to my life. He simply brought life *to my life*! It wasn't intentional, but I made him my god.

Love hurts.

I woke up countless mornings searching for my cell phone that was hidden in the sheets. The love pains were sometimes unbearable and most of the time indescribable when there were no calls or text messages from him. Every other minute, throughout the day, I checked my phone and waited for him to reach out to me. Nothing. Whenever I called or texted, he didn't always answer. However, when I was around him, his phone was glued to his hands. *Hmph!*

Love hurts.

He constantly complimented me, bought me things, cooked for me, and even granted me access to some of his confidential belongings. But for some reason, when I inquired about *us* and asked what we were doing, he pushed back and said things like,

"What are you talking about? We're just friends," or,

"Why are you reading so much into this?"

He said last summer that he wasn't ready to be in a relationship, but I wondered why we did things as if we were a couple.

Love hurts.

Of all the relationships I've experienced, this man showed me that he cared for me on numerous occasions. Maybe, just maybe, love hurts because all the other men told me that they loved me, but never showed me.

Love hurts. ·

Someone once said, "The only way to get over a man is to get under another one." That's a lie! It didn't work for me because during dinner with the new guy, I only thought about cutting the date short. I couldn't wait to see the man that caused my love pains, all the while knowing that he wasn't trying to make time to see *me*.

Love hurts.

A mutual friend of ours asked, "If he called at 3 o'clock in the morning, stranded, would you go get him?" Without hesitation, I immediately said yes! Then he asked, "If God told you to give all your worries to Him and let this man go, would you do it?" There was complete silence.

Love hurts.

I'm not a drinker, not even socially, but I sipped a glass of Moscato and hoped that the love pains would evaporate. Instead, they worsened. They got worse because the truth is that he was just not feeling me.

Love hurts.

A year later and I know I lost myself in that man. The pains I experienced moved through my body and made it difficult to navigate throughout the day.

Someday I hope to answer that God question with an honest answer. Right now, though, love hurts.

Tonya is a single black woman from Arkansas. She is currently seeking her Masters Degree in business administration. She enjoys reading, shopping, networking, listening to different genres of music, cooking, playing golf and working-out. One of her favorite quotes is, "When someone shows you who they are, believe them the first time." –Maya Angelou

Wait on the Lord

By Rev. Kia, *Free*

The time was 9:43pm. I had just looked through an album of a friend of mine who had been married for almost two years and celebrated the birth of her beautiful daughter. I cried.

Please don't misunderstand me. I was really happy for her and had prayed God's blessings over her marriage and her precious seed, but I thought, *Where is mine*?! I had been in a love-limbo-purgatory-roller-coaster-chaotic-manic depression for the past two years. There were days when I was elated with my life, the state of my heart, my career, my ministry that meets the hearts of hundreds or more daily, and with my God. And then, there were days when my only solace was tucked away in the middle of my bed. The only way that I could have peace was to curl up as closely as I could get to that spot and cry, twisted in a ball of self-pity.

I found myself there one night. I remembered the man that I loved more than any other on earth. The man who used his ministry to lure me in used his flesh to blindfold me to his deception. He later left me jilted at the prophetic altar that he promised me. He also said that I was his God-given wife and I believed him. I thought that God was in agreement, even months after he became verbally abusive and neglectful. Eventually, he got another woman pregnant. We had been broken up for almost a year when I learned of the child, but it stung like our love was still bliss.

The entire time God knew what I needed to draw me closer to my purpose. He had to hit me with the most unsuspected blow, so that when I fell to my knees, I fell at His feet! Now, I know what I deserve. I know what I desire. And, I trust in the divine to lead me to my husband.

Whenever I think of the things that I know God has promised me: an international ministry, a loving husband, and beautiful children, I hold fast to my favorite scripture. In the gospel of Luke 1:45, Elizabeth tells Mary, mother of Jesus, one of the most powerful prophecies proclaimed in the Bible. She says, "And blessed is *she* that *believed:* for there *shall* be a *performance* of those things which were *told* her from the *Lord*!"

Every woman reading may not be pregnant with the messiah as Mary was in the Gospel of Luke, but we are all impregnated with God's promises. As Elizabeth reminds Mary, I remind you. If God promised it, it shall be performed. A performance requires an audience and it requires preparation. The people in your life will be watching God operate through you and thus, you need to get ready!

Seek God while he prepares your love.

We are all mothers of love. We must nourish it, birth it, and protect it. Only then will God send us someone to raise our love with.

Rev. Kia, MA, is the first female licensed to preach the gospel at a church founded by slaves in Memphis. An alumna of both Clark Atlanta University and the University of Chicago, Kia is a supervisor for foster parent recruiting in all of West Tennessee. She is an artist, poet, writer, founder, mentor and most of all, a servant.

All Yoked Up!

By Alacia, *Free*

*"Be ye not unequally yoked together with unbelievers:
for what fellowship hath righteousness with
unrighteousness? and what communion hath light with
darkness?"*

- 2 Corinthians 6:14

About two years ago, I thought that I caught a glimpse of my future. I began dating a man whom I considered to be "The One." He had it all. He was, all clichés aside, "tall, dark, and handsome." He didn't come with kids, criminal records, or drama. He had a good job, came from a good family, and was financially stable. We had a story-book relationship. Of course, things weren't perfect, but for the most part, we were happy. We rarely ever fought, and when we did, we resolved it in a respectful, mature way. On top of all that, we were friends, finish-each-other's-sentences friends. Things were going great. I just knew that this was my husband.

I have purposely left out one very important bit of information about this man, a fact that—had I taken this as seriously as I knew I should have upon discovery—would have prevented an enormous amount of pain, suffering, and confusion for both parties. This man was not saved. There it is: the ugly truth. And I knew it immediately. I also knew that no matter how cute people said we were or how good it felt to be with him, the relationship was wrong. It was not founded on Godly principles, and despite all my efforts to dress it up, bringing him to church, visiting the parents, praying that God would save him, God was nowhere in it.

Why did I continue the relationship, knowing that we were unequally yoked? Well, I fell into the same traps that entice many singles. My first problem was that in my arrogance and impatience, I did what I was supposed to allow God to do. I went out and found that man. I actually made a decision upon meeting him that if I found myself back in South Georgia after graduation, I was going to find and marry him. I was accustomed to always getting what/who I wanted, so when I got saved, I carried that same attitude about dating and marriage. I was aware that God intended for man to find his wife, but I thought that since the ratio of single black, professional, men to women of the same demographic was disproportionate, I should help my husband find me, regardless of whether he was looking or not.

Secondly, I was disobedient. I could clearly hear God say, "Get out of that relationship." I just wouldn't listen. I stayed in it and ultimately crossed boundaries that should have never been approached, causing major spiritual and emotional battles.

Finally, I gave into loneliness. When I left the city, I knew that my social life would change because of the cultural gap between city and rural living;

however, I was enormously ill-prepared for what moving back would be like. I really felt like a fish out of water because a majority of my peers were now parents or spouses. Furthermore, being surrounded with images of family life, I got lonely. God gave me other options, though. He always had me surrounded with people I could have reached out to. Instead, I reached for a man, and that's when I stepped out of God's plan for my life.

For two to three years, I struggled with lust, fornication, and spiritual turmoil. I had my man, though, and that was all that mattered. I risked my opportunity for eternal life for fleeting, pseudo-gratification. Ironically, I never really felt satisfied, even with "Mr. Perfect." I just told myself that he was as close to my "Mr. Right" as I was going to get. I was afraid to let him go because I didn't want to have to face the fact that I might have to wait a long time before God actually sent my man. I was actually prepared to marry that unsaved man and deal with the consequences rather than face singleness.

God didn't let that happen though. I thank Him so much for His unrelenting Holy Spirit. He kept convicting me for my sin in that relationship until I literally couldn't take it anymore. I said to Him one afternoon in repentance, "Lord, You know I'm not going to let this man go on my own, so You're going to have to do it for me." I won't get into all the details of the breakup, but God opened my eyes long enough and wide enough to see just how wrong my "Mr. Right" was. God showed me that when it comes to a husband, being a good man just isn't enough. I want and deserve a Godly man. This decision wasn't easy, but I refused to allow my fleshly desires to convince me to marry someone that God had not purposed for me. The Bible clearly instructs, "Husbands, love your wives, just as Christ also loved the church and gave Himself up for her" (Ephesians 5:25). Now how can he love me like Christ if he doesn't know Christ?

I thank God for the revelation He has given me through this process and I am definitely not willing to put myself or another man through more emotional catharsis simply because I want a "boo." This time, I'll wait because I know that God is pleased with my obedience and my sacrifice.

Moreover, I am sure that He has a greater reward waiting for me, not just the best husband ever, but the confidence in knowing that because I have put my trust in Him, regarding this matter, I am that much closer to abundant living on Earth and eternal bliss with Him in heaven.

Alacia is a graduate of Clark Atlanta University and fourth-year English teacher at Thomas County Central High School in Thomasville, Georgia. Although she enjoys teaching and embracing responsibility to her students, her real passion is music. She completed her debut gospel album, Passionate Praise, which was released in summer 2010. Despite numerous struggles, she is learning to welcome the challenges of singleness and take advantage of the numerous opportunities for ministry that are placed before her.

Love and Know Yourself

By Yashica, *Free*

"My lover is mine, and I am his;"

-Song of Solomon 2:16

I've been single a little over two years now. Some would assume that I am unhappy because I am alone, but honestly, I am happier than I have ever been in my life.

I'm at a point to where my spiritual relationship with God is stronger. I can say that I love who I am—the good, the great, the bad, and the ugly. Being single has shown me what love is. For that, I truly have greater desires in life and love. Being single has shown me how to conquer trials without distractions. Yes, I do get lonely sometimes, but I know that I'm never alone. God is with me.

Being single has also revealed that many people in my circle of friends and family are afraid to be alone. They're afraid of the silence. They fear that they'd have to deal with themselves. Many of those same people have told me that I am closing myself off to the possibility of falling in love. I beg to differ. I feel I was always open to falling in love, but mainly because of a void. Much of that void had to do with the double-dutch relationship that I had with my father, my inconsistent relationship with GOD, and my lack of self-love. I fell for any and everything that looked like the love I had been programmed to believe in, which was never real love.

Being single has allowed me to reevaluate what a God-fearing relationship is and how to maintain it. I've learned how to treat others, but most of all, I've learned how to treat myself. I now teach people how to love *me* better. I believe the man that God has will be for me. He will come when God feels that I'm ready. I truly believe that the woman is never to look for her man...he is to look for her. She is to position herself for him when God says it's time. Until then, it's important for me to make a life of my own before trying to build one with someone else.

These two years have been an enormous spiritual and emotional journey that only God can create. He has given me an eternal joy, peace, and love. Nothing can come between me and the relationship that I have with my number one man, God!

To the single women who feel that they need to have a man in their lives to fit into this man-made mold of what's important, you don't *need* anyone! You need to love *yourself.* You need to live out your purpose and keep God first! Once you get your priorities where they should be, the man that you want will come. The purpose that you serve will blossom. God will keep everything afloat. Don't look to others to define what happiness, peace, or joy is for you. To find happiness, you need God and you *must* know who you are!

Yashica is a graduate of Clark Atlanta University and currently editing her first novel. Yashica recently stepped out on faith and relocated to San Francisco, California to attend graduate school for marriage and family therapy. In her spare time, she loves to read, write, paint, listen to music, workout, and daydream.

The Fight to Love

By Courtney P., *Free*

"I beseech you therefore, brethren, by the mercies of God, that ye present your bodies a living sacrifice, holy, acceptable unto God, which is your reasonable service."

-Romans 12:1

I met this amazing person who was a joy to be around. She loved everything that I loved and hated everything that I hated. She laughed when I laughed and cried when I cried. This wonderful person loved what I looked like in the morning *and* night. Loving her became so easy.

For a while, I couldn't appreciate her. I couldn't stand her existence. I wanted her dead, so I would do things to show her how much I disliked her. There were times when I would watch as men took advantage of her body. I would stand by and watch as she gave herself to men that had no desire of ever making her their queen. I would stare as she allowed men to enter and exit her personal glory. Her excuses would be,

"He bought me dinner,"

"He traveled far," or,

"He gave me gas money."

I stood by as she went to church. The same men that abused her mentally, sexually, and emotionally, were in the same room shouting, "Preach, Bishop," or preaching themselves. I witnessed her leave church services looking beautiful on the outside, but having no clue of how unhealthy she was on the inside. I can attest to her fading away. She no longer cared about her appearance. She couldn't stand to be alone. She felt like no one cared about her.

Finally, she realized how poor her condition was. She was reminded that she didn't need anyone to affirm her identity. She picked up the word of God and it read, "To all who mourn in Israel, [Hebrew in Zion], he will give a crown of beauty for ashes, a joyous blessing instead of mourning, festive praise instead of despair. In their righteousness, they will be like great oaks that the Lord has planted for his own glory" (Isaiah 61:3). She could see that she had a purpose and a reason for living.

That woman that I once hated was *me*.

Despite the breakups and heartaches experienced in the name of love, I have acquired a life lesson. I learned that Jesus is the ultimate sacrifice. I should no longer feel the need to sacrifice myself (identity, likes, dislikes, etc.). We are all called to love from a God-fearing, unconditional place. We must know and embrace the true love of God. God's love never fails. His love heals, endures, suffers long , it is kind, meek, thoughtful, and selfless. Before I am able to love anyone else, I must love God and myself. Now I get it!

Why was it that I felt like I owed every man that wanted any parts of me sexually or mentally? I came to this conclusion when an ex called me. My ex was in town for a funeral, so we talked briefly on the phone before he came into town. He called once he arrived. I didn't want to answer the phone because I had finally gotten to a place where men were not on my mind. I wanted to focus on me and get over the hurt from a recent breakup. That old feeling of owing someone returned and I answered the phone.

He asked if he could crash on my couch for the evening because he didn't have a place to stay. I told him that was okay. When he had gotten to my place, we talked and caught up on the old times. When it was time to sleep, I threw him a blanket, turned off the lights, and said good night. I headed to my bed to read and as I was engrossed in my book, I heard him say, "Thanks a lot."

"You're welcome," I said sarcastically.

He says it again.

I then get up and ask, "Are you comfortable?"

"I will manage. Come here."

I bashfully walked over to the couch. He then goes for a kiss. In that moment, I absolutely had no desire to kiss him or do anything, but again I felt like I owed him because he had traveled from Chicago. I tried to use every excuse I could imagine, but they didn't work.

I dropped him off at the airport the next day. We rode in silence. I'm sure we both could agree that it was not good that we'd reintroduced ourselves. He turned to me and asked if I was mad at him. I replied with a cold response, "No."

To be honest, I was mad that I let him come back into my life for that moment. The truth was that I was upset with myself for all the years of saying yes and feeling like I owed men my *body*. The Bible says, "I beseech you therefore, brethren, by the mercies of God, that ye present your bodies a living sacrifice, holy, acceptable unto God, *which is* your reasonable service" (Romans 12:1). That scripture is a clear indicator that Jesus gave his life, so the least we can do is present ourselves to God.

I finally understood that my problem was deep. I didn't love myself, so that ultimately lead me to question, *Did I love God?* I had to immediately repent to God first for not loving Him as I should have as well as myself.

I can honestly say that that was the first day that I became *super single*! I now enjoy being by myself because I learned how to love God with my mind, body, and soul. I truly learned how to love myself. The second step for me was forgiving myself and forgiving the men who misused and abused me. I had to forgive and let go.

Today, I challenge you to learn the power of the word "no." Realize how precious you are. Once you realize your value, you won't allow anyone or yourself to tear you down and make you feel like you are less than anything. You are fearfully and wonderfully made by God. Once you accept Christ into your life, He lives in you.

Imagine that you are allowing people to disrespect the place where God lives. Decide today that you will no longer be a part of anything that will disrespect your Creator and what He has done for you. God loves you today. While you are a *super single*, I challenge you to get extremely close to Him so you can learn how to truly love and be loved.

Courtney P. was raised in Powder Springs, Georgia. Her parents, Rev. Patrick and Tanya Phillips raised her in the admonition of the Lord. Courtney attended The University of West Georgia where she majored in Mass Communications with a minor in Theatre. Courtney has a passion for Christ and making his love known through singing. Courtney lives by the thought , "I can be changed by what happens to me, but I refuse to be reduced by it." -Maya Angelou

Through the Storm

By Brenda, *Divorced*

"And this is my prayer: I pray that you love more and more. I pray that you will have better understanding and be wise in all things."

-Philippians 1:9

I got married at an early age—17, to be exact. I stayed married for 23 years. I thought that my life was pretty stress-free. I didn't have any problems. I loved my husband. He was a good man, good husband, good provider, and a very good father. I was spoiled. I didn't work at all and was a house wife until he decided to cheat on me. Two years before my husband walked out of my life, I had just joined the church. Knowing the Lord is what has kept me sane. My ex-husband's walking out of my life was Storm #1.

The Lord gave me a second chance, however. I dated a Christian man and we were both hurting in the same way. His wife had also walked out and left him, but with two sons to raise. I felt that God brought us together. We dated for a few years when he decided to ask me to marry him. I was thrilled!

We got married on August 20, 1995.

I know we had a Christian marriage. We prayed together, laughed together, and went to church together. We genuinely loved one another. As time went on, my mom was unable to stay alone, so he and I discussed moving her in with us. I loved my mother so much and decided to take her in.

There was a lot of stress between us afterwards. We began to fall apart. One thing led to another and I decided to call it quits. We went to our pastor, but I didn't listen. When I finally did decide to listen, it was too late. I filed for a separation and it turned out to be a divorce. Storm #2.

He and I stayed at the same church for 5 years. He sat on the left side and I sat on the right. I never looked that way, either. During this time, I stayed faithful to God. I was a bit ashamed, but I knew that He still loved me. He just hated my divorce. Our pastor had a series on divorce one Sunday. He talked about breaking God's covenant and how much he hated divorces.

One day, I got a letter in the mail at my home for me and my ex-husband to go to a graduation. I normally wouldn't call him, but this time I did. His number was still the same. I left a message and he later returned my call. The rest is history.

We now know the cause of the problem. Today, we are friends and God allowed us to sit in the center pews from our years to now. Only God can bring people's lives back together. I feel so blessed and still ask for God's directions. We never stopped having the love that we shared in that 7 ½ years. I know that I made a big mistake and I asked God for forgiveness. I tell all sisters to hang in there and don't do anything that you know will be regretted.

Brenda was born in Buffalo, NY. She describes herself as a" God-fearing woman who loves the Lord" and is grateful to have been saved for over 20 years. She enjoys caring for the elderly, spending time with her grandchildren, bowling, interior decorating, and reading her favorite book, the Holy Bible. *Her favorite scripture is, "I can do all things through Christ, who strengthens me" (Philippians 4:13).*

Worth the Wait

By Vannessa, *Coupled*

"For I know the plans I have for you," declares the LORD, "plans to prosper you and not to harm you, plans to give you hope and a future."

–Jeremiah 29:11

We live in a world where society dictates the standards of relationships and life in general. Books bash us [women], celebrities treat us like sex objects, songs devalue relationships, and women are lowering the bar every day— just to get or keep a man. Through my most painful and desperate times, I began to become the virtuous woman God longed for me to be. I encourage you to walk away from all toxic relationships and don't look back. I hope and pray that you find inner strength that comes from God. With that being said, I think I will call this...worth the wait.

I have never been happier than I am now. For the first time at 29, I am in an adult relationship. I am thankful to God for creating an amazing man, but above all for allowing me to be ready for this relationship. After so many struggles, I decided that I was not going to allow the devil to run or ruin my relationship. It was not going to be based solely on looks, status, or all the things we think make us happy, but on something deeper and more meaningful, such as his relationship with God.

In the past, I often told myself that maybe if I lowered my standards, it would work. I compromised when I knew what the word of God said. I was Mrs. Fix It, though. I just needed more time to *change* him. I had to prove a point!

Sex isn't everything. I realized that the day I sat outside a male friend's house crying in my car. He was telling me that our friendship couldn't last because I didn't want to have sex with him. I was devastated. I was tired of having to be the pretty girl and the scorned woman. I was sick of being unhappy. As I cried, I said, "Lord, I want to do right, but with the men that are in my life, I can't do it." I cried and cried. I drove away with tear-stained clothes and began to talk to God, as if He were sitting beside me. I threw my hands up and surrendered because I knew that this was bigger and much deeper then I could handle on my own. I was sick of the masquerade and sick of pretending. I needed real help and not the kind of help that would come from a TV show or magazine. I needed help from God and a strong circle of family and friends.

A few months later, I met a man that God designed for me. The best thing is that I have not had to compromise my faith, intelligence, or body. I can finally be me and experience a God-driven relationship. I am not bragging, but I think that our faith, trust in God, and each other keeps us together. I know God is pleased with our relationship and for that, I am thankful. Surrendering to God and walking away from the drama has been one of the best moves I've made.

This is one of the biggest lessons I have learned as a single woman: don't compromise to the point where you lose your identity. Think about it, do you really want to be with someone who makes demands, but refuses to change to suit *your* needs?

Vannessa graduated from the University of Houston and currently attends the University of Phoenix. When she is not planning an event or writing press information, she enjoys traveling and being with family and friends. She loves reading, volunteering, shopping, and going to church.

In the Meantime

Aletha, *Free*

Sunset. Flowers. Candlelight dinner. Wine. Perfume. Soft music. Sweet words whispered in your ear.

"It's not you. It's me."

It's over. You cry. He runs. Denial turns to anger—anger turns to confusion.

"Why me? Why again?"

Your friends tell you that he is coming back and you believe them.

Weeks turn to months. Mornings are unbearable. Nights are unheard of. You seek refuge in other men. You feel dirty...more pain, more regrets, more alcohol, more parties, more men. Bitter prayers turn to no prayers at all. Denial makes you believe that you don't need a man. Time and prayer heals your heart. You find yourself again, love yourself again, and you are single...again.

Contrary to popular belief, you are not *single* if you are still struggling with the idea of the other person moving on, loving someone else and continuing his/her life without you. If you are still overwhelmed with emotion at the thought of him or the sound of his name, you are still mentally *attached* and it will be unfair to the other person you date to bring this baggage to the next relationship. It's okay to be sad. But like my good friend candidly told me during my most painful breakup, "You can't be bitter. God needs you to be the happy person you are. So does the next guy you date or your future husband."

In the meantime—the time between the end of one relationship and the beginning of another—can be a time of reflection, self discovery, or a time of bitterness, regrets, and revenge. I think I slept through most of my "in the meantime," but, my hindsight is so much clearer now. If the now me could go back the heartbroken hot mess, laying-in-bed-all-day-trying-to-figure-out-what-went-wrong me self, this is what I would of given myself to read (because she loves lists and they are so much easier to read):

Get *up* and *out*...every day. It's so much easier said than done, but your heart is in survival mode and you need to get out of your apartment. Go anywhere. Just get out.

I was in a new city during my breakup, so I didn't have any close friends or family at the time. On the days I dragged myself out of bed (I was actually sleeping on the floor because I had just moved here), I would spend time driving around the city, thinking and looking around. Then I would go back home. I did feel a little better.

Get dressed. Get pretty. Make yourself feel good. Get your toes done...your hair...your nails. Make sure that you are making a effort to look your best every day. Looking good makes you feel

good, feeling good makes you happy, and happy heals the heart. Do something that you did before you got into a relationship.

For me, it was music. I listened to music that reminded me of my life before I was in a relationship.

Don't think, just do. Do whatever it is that you couldn't do while in the relationship. Travel. Dance in the apartment naked, anything. Make goals.

Making goals distracts you long enough for you to focus on something else.

The year after pulling myself out of the rut I was in, I started making lists of things that I wanted to do for the day, month, and even the year. I kept track of my progress, too.

It's been 3 years now and I've accomplished so much. I'm happy with myself and have made myself better. You can do this, too.

Philippians 3:12-14 reads, "Not that I have already obtained all this, or have already been made perfect, but I press on to take hold of that for which Christ Jesus took hold of me. Brothers, I do not consider myself yet to have taken hold of it. But one thing I do: Forgetting what is behind and straining toward what is ahead, I press on toward the goal to win the prize for which God has called me heavenward in Christ Jesus."

Aletha is a fairly smart woman who just so happened to go through a painful breakup in the past so that she could give candid advice to women who are in the midst of a breakdown. She currently lives in Ohio, working on her masters in Chemical Engineering and starting a cosmetic line. She spends every morning thanking God and dancing in the mirror.

What Are You Doing?

By Sonya, *Free*

I give all honor and glory to God for me being a 36-year-old virgin.

I'm going to cut straight to the chase:

Do I get tired of being alone? Yes, especially in the spring and summer.

Have I gotten tired of waiting on a husband? Yes.

Have I gotten mad at God for taking too long to send my husband? Yes.

It is funny when we think God wears a watch. It is even funnier when we think that the omnipresent, omnipotent, and omniscient God is subject to our timeline. *So how did I move on from my complaining and whining? I grew up. I matured.*

We mess up by focusing on a man and not focusing on The Man. God wants us for His glory. We need to put more attention on His will for our lives as opposed to,

"God I'm tired of being by myself."

"Sally Ann has a man and I don't."

"God I'm lonely."

"God I'm almost 30 and still single."

"God all my friends are married except me."

God doesn't inhabit our complaints, but our praises. The truth is that if God sent you a husband right now, you wouldn't be ready. How do I know? If you are complaining, anxious, mad, discouraged, and lonely, then you are not ready. Your focus is in the wrong place. God is waiting on a mature bride. Have you ever thought that you're not waiting on God, but that God is waiting on you? "For I know the plans I have for you," says the LORD. "They are plans for good and not for disaster, to give you a future and a hope. In those days when you pray, I will listen. If you look for me wholeheartedly, you will find me." (Jeremiah 29:11-13, NLT). Seek God, not a husband.

What do we do, while we wait for our Boaz? Let us look at Ruth. "One day Ruth the Moabite said to Naomi, "Let me go out into the harvest fields to pick up the stalks of grain left behind by anyone who is kind enough to let me do it." Naomi replied, "All right, my daughter, go ahead"(Ruth 2:2, NLT). Ruth was in the field minding her own business working. Ruth also was humble and picked up the leftovers. She was submissive to Naomi. To submit means to obey. Are you being obedient to God's call on your life?

What are you working on that God has called you to do? In other words, what is your purpose? If you don't know it, I suggest that you begin finding it by fasting and praying. If you find yourself asking God, "What have you brought to birth?" (Isaiah 45:10, NIV), then it's more than important to have an answer. If you know your purpose and are not working on it, then what are you waiting on?

Sonya Waddell is a Mental Health Therapist, works in the school setting, and loves to write. She released her first book in Fall 2010 entitled, Single Ladies: Living Holy in a Sexy World. *In her spare time, she loves to dance, travel, cook, and spend time with loved ones.*

Be Still

By Judé, *Free*

"Be still," He said. "What are you doing looking for that special someone?"

"God, I'm ready for a man all my own," I replied.

"Work." He said. "While you're handling *my* business, I'll take good care of yours."

"God, what will you have me to do?"

"Be quiet," He said. "I've allowed the unexpected, unimaginable, and the abnormal to happen to humble and strengthen you. Listen up! For I'm depositing into your spirit all that you will need to handle *my* business. I've sent people in and out of your life to *stir up* the gift that I've placed within you."

"God I don't want to do this by myself. I need male companionship. I get lonely when everyone's around. I desire to be held and only a real man can hold me down. I want to hear, 'I love you,' at the drop of a dime. I desire to be kissed and everyone make me smile—"

"Stop! Don't you know I love you? Have you considered me? I've been waiting patiently and you always overlook me. I guess because you can't feel, touch, or kiss me. To you, I'm not *real* enough. But I'm the realest you'll ever know. I get frustrated when all the attributes you look for in a man describe just a portion of me...."

I sit back and wonder why can't she see?

I am love, the word defined.

All that you're looking for is in Me

And even though you can't see Me, I'm always there loving on you.

And you don't even care.

I wake you every morning and lay with you at night.

I protect you and make everything alright.

I'm jealous, so I don't want you with just any man.

I want you with someone who is just like Me, who will love you unconditionally.

The love I have for you, you will never understand.

So just for you, I've created a man.

And he will know who you are.

You're the missing part of him, just beneath his arms,

You create a protective barrier around his lungs, liver, and heart.

The missing rib is who you are.

You are his protective barrier.

You shield his lungs, which is how I gave him My spirit.

You protect his liver which filters out waste

and you protect his heart which is the wellspring of life.

"Be still," He said.

"You don't have to strategically place yourself anywhere.

Your man will know, himself.

"Work," He said.

"While you're in the fields working, your BOAZ will see you from afar off

"Be quiet," He says.

So you can hear him when he calls you.

Listen up! So you can hear *Me* speaking through *him.*

Stop! So that you can see that the man I created you for you

Is just a physical representation of *He* which is *me.*

He will come no sooner than I say, so you may as well get busy.

While you're working, your mate is on the way.

He'll find you when you least expect it,

but when He comes you'll know.

It'll be the still small voice that reminds you that the bible told you so.

11And that, knowing the time, that now it is high time to awake out of sleep: for now is our salvation nearer than when we believed. 12 The night is far spent, the day is at hand: let us therefore cast off the works of darkness, and let us put on the armour of light.

13 Let us walk honestly, as in the day; not in rioting and drunkenness, not in chambering and wantonness, not in strife and envying. 14 But put ye on the Lord Jesus Christ, and make not provision for the flesh, to fulfill the lusts thereof.

Judé is the eldest of six children. She prays that her endeavors will inspire and uplift other young ladies in the situations she has overcome. She hopes that those who have made it through will speak up and know that they are not worthless, but priceless! She enjoys singing, reading, writing, and spending time with friends and family.

Because We Are Beautiful

By Ashley W., *Free*

I must admit that being single is a challenge, especially at an age where everyone seems to be finding "the one" all around you. Seasoned married people will constantly tell you not to rush or settle. Since some have been together for 10+ years and still prefer one another's company above all, I think they know what they are talking about.

During this time of singleness, I am learning more about myself and working toward being who God wants me to be in every area of my life. I am the type of person that does not like the hassle of wasting time, bouncing from relationship-to-relationship. I generally keep it casual. I have had a couple of serious relationships prior to this drought and in all I honesty, what I've learned from them is exactly what I do *not* want. I am not sure if I needed to go through them to learn lessons, either. They created a wall around my heart and made me bitter, which not only affected other romantic relationships, but friendships as well. Now, with the help of the Holy Spirit, I am trying to break down the walls so that when God does bring my man along, I will be receptive to him.

1 Corinthians 7:32-34 reads, "I want you to be free from the concerns of this life. An unmarried man can spend his time doing the Lord's work and

thinking how to please him. But a married man has to think about his earthly responsibilities and how to please his wife. His interests are divided..." I know that at this time in my life, there is so much more that God wants from me. At one point, my thoughts were so consumed with finding a man that I needed to check myself. I know that when I am completely in love with my Lord and Savior Jesus Christ, the right man that He has chosen will find me.

We must remain pure and prepare our hearts and minds for our man. This is a time where I am enjoying life to the fullest with no strings attached. If I want to take a trip on short notice, I do not have to consult with anyone first, although my mom still likes to be included in my plans.

When God is first, the sky isn't the limit. My possibilities exceed the sky. I am enjoying these moments with myself, my family, and friends. I know that God will bring my mate along. Esther 2:12 says, "Before each young woman was taken to the king's bed, she was given the prescribed twelve months of beauty treatments..." Like Esther had to prepare a whole year for her one night with the king, I am taking this time to prepare for my king. I am not doing that by dating around, but by seeking God's will for me, allowing him to heal my heart, making sure I am beautiful on the inside and outside, and having the time of my life by doing what makes me happy. I look forward to the day when my next journey begins with my hubby, my best friend, my lover.

Ashley W. graduated from the University of Houston with a Bachelor of Science in psychology. She currently works as a research coordinator at Baylor College of Medicine on several genetic research studies that look for genes associated with congenital defects. She loves Jesus and enjoys hanging out with friends and family, traveling, movies, dancing, eating, sleeping, the beach, and art.

After the Exam

By Lucretia, *Free*

"For I know the thoughts that I think toward you, saith the LORD, thoughts of peace, and not of evil, to give you an expected end."

-Jeremiah 29:11

Fill in the blank: I have to _____ by the age of 30.

We make this full shopping list of career goals, vacation spots to visit, famous people to meet, marriage, and kids all in order, as if life is going downhill right after 30. Some of us may create this list at different stages of our lives such as after high school, college graduation, or at the pinnacle point of transformation. As a social networker, I constantly notice multiple status updates of wedding engagements, videos of men proposing to their ladies, and pictures of wedding ceremonies. Overload! Sometimes we take a flight to Dream Land and imagine ourselves in these moments of happiness. As we slowly travel back to earth, we realize that we're still single! Nothing has changed. Our left hand bears no weight and we are not in a relationship. *What happened? We had life mapped out, right?*

Of course, I'm not the only one that made this mistake, but at some point we all do it. Worry and fear finally settled in me as years went by and I realized at the age of 25 that I had no idea where my life was headed. I thought, *Is something missing?* One moment I felt secure with my plans and being single. Next, I'm headed into depression. Chocolates, romance novels, and chick flicks could not cure the insecurities that brewed inside of me. *Where was all this sparking from?*

I took the time to examine my past, myself, and the little girl I closed the door to a while ago. I resisted confronting the girl who stood in front of the mirror with her eyes closed. The little girl who tried to alter her physical features from her nose to her toes, her hair, her teeth, her eyes, and her skin. Although she was loved and called beautiful by her parents, this did not compare to the weapons of hurtful words that had absorbed into the pits of her soul.

That little girl was me and I didn't embrace my true beauty. As I grew up, acceptance was the latest trend. I wasn't popular, was never asked out by the cutest guy on campus, nor did I receive personal invites to parties. I chose to hide my anxiety and depression. I placed a Band-Aid over my scars and aspired for higher education and other school activities. As I matured, I dated, made new friends, became a part of a sorority, involved myself in the ministry, and later, my career. I became a pro at replacing voids and hiding the true woman that nobody really knew. *Check! This was my plan!*

For me, I never really had much luck in the dating department. I encountered my first relationship my junior year in college. My guard was let down with him and we were inseparable. *Yes! Bingo!* I knew for sure he would be the addition to my goal list! *Check!* But, long-story-short, he broke my heart and I lost the scapegoat to all my insecurities. I was left standing in the mirror once again? Empty. My plan failed.

After close examination, I couldn't even recognize the real me. This list that I created was bursting out of control. I came to the conclusion, that God's purpose and plan was never incorporated into my goals. I found false validation and placed limits on God. My plans and list couldn't categorize the will that God had for me. See, I allowed God to help me to be comfortable with all of me: my beauty, inside-and-out. I became secure with the little girl that I had never reached out to. I began to trust and love God more for the future that I would soon encounter.

Remember, we are not in competition with our peers. Everyone's will for everyone varies. We forget that God is preparing us for a special someone willing to love our past, open our present, and be there for our future. God is also preparing *him* for *you*. Take a walk with our Creator to aid your insecurities. Let Him be the passenger for your new level of satisfaction in becoming a single, purified, and patient woman of God. So, don't throw away your list. Substitute it for God's and let Him take control.

Lucretia is a graduate of Clark Atlanta University. She resides in Kansas City, Kansas, where she is the co-founder and program coordinator of Youth City Network. She loves poetry, listening to music, traveling, spending time with family, and finding new ways to inspire youth.

The Next Test

By Shaka, *Free*

I heard God's voice clearly. He said to me, "Shaka, when I put a good man in your life don't go looking elsewhere." I heard him, but it was too late, that good man had moved on and there was nothing I could do to bring him back.

My story begins in January 2008. I'd moved to a new city for a job. In this city, I met a man who was not "Shaka's type" at first glance. He wasn't 6 feet, but he was taller than me. He wasn't drop-dead handsome, but he caught my attention. He was nearly three years my junior, but mature enough to hold a conversion with the best. He was a good man.

Within weeks, this man became my man. He asked me to be his girlfriend. I can't recall the last time someone had actually asked me to be their girlfriend. I was impressed. I liked him and wanted a fresh start.

The relationship wasn't perfect, but it wasn't awful either. He treated me with love and respect. In a way, he reminded me of my late father. His qualities were that of a man I could see myself loving, marrying, and starting a family with.

We maintained the relationship for over a year. It wasn't perfect, but it wasn't awful either. I loved this man. He loved me more, but I couldn't stop thinking of my ex who was back in Atlanta. The devil was busy.

I'd occasionally speak to this ex. He had a girlfriend and I had my boyfriend, so it was just *talk*. I started to think of the what-if's. These thoughts flooded my brain and eventually my heart. I began to start pulling away from my boyfriend.

It was in February 2009, one month after I celebrated my one-year anniversary with my boyfriend that the same boyfriend—who forgot it was our anniversary and later remembered—rushed to Edible Arrangements to order me a lovely fruit arrangement. He wasn't perfect, but he wasn't awful either.

In February, I attended the funeral of my cousin's mother. Funerals will make you put your own life in perspective. Just a month earlier, my uncle unexpectedly passed and less than two years before that, my father passed. I remember sitting there thinking that I didn't want to live the rest of my life, however long or short it would be, wondering— living a what-if life.

I then decided to be honest with the ex and tell him that I still had these feelings for him, so I did. However, I didn't break up with my boyfriend and he didn't break up with his girlfriend.

I didn't break up with my current boyfriend, but I remember making the relationship very difficult. We argued more when we lived together, which was a suggestion he made after my hours were cut to part-time. He didn't want me to struggle, so he moved in and we split the bills. After all, we were sure that we would get married anyway. What an awesome gesture from an awesome man! Too bad I didn't show my appreciation. Sure, I said thank you, but my actions said why are you here? I continued to make the relationship difficult until we finally broke up in April 2009.

We continued to live together because we were still friends. Finally, I felt free enough to pursue the ex in Atlanta. Something in my spirit didn't feel right, though. I always felt uneasy about rekindling anything with him. The thrill wasn't gone, but it sure wasn't the same thrill as before.

Meanwhile, my new ex was still my *roommate.* We still went out and did other things together. The love was still there. There were times I'd look at him and know without a doubt that this man still loved me. I knew that all I had to do was say the word and he'd be willing to give us another try. He even asked me one time to try again and I said no. At the same time, my friends and family are telling me how good this man was and how much they loved and adored him. My grandma still wanted to send him biscuits. I couldn't have a conversation with anyone in my family without them asking me about him.

My spirit told me to reconsider. *He's a good man. Your family loves him, you still love him, and God loves him for you. He's not perfect, but he's not awful, either.* I ignored my spirit. I ignored everything inside of my heart and soul and followed the false feelings that went through my body and head.

By the time I was ready to listen, it was too late. All of summer 2009, I struggled with my feelings.

I was so close to following my heart and asking him to try again. Even when he joined a dating website and begin to date I knew deep in my heart that he still loved me. All I had to do was say, "Baby, let's try again. We're not perfect, but we're not awful, and I know God will not let us fail." My heart said all these things, but my pride would never let the words leave my mouth.

By September, he met the girl he really liked and for the first time, I felt threatened. Normally, I'm not easily shaken. I finally put my pride aside and told him exactly how I felt. His response was, "Why now? It's too late."

I was devastated, but felt I still had a chance. I thought, *Okay. This is just some girl he's dating. How far could an online relationship go? She lives out-of-state and there are so many odds against them.* But the relationship lasted through September.

By mid-September, I started losing my faith. I was a wreck. The pain was more than unbearable. I stopped eating, not because I wanted to, but because I had no appetite. Within three weeks, I'd gone from 140 pounds to 123 and by the time October rolled around, I was down to 120. I cried all the time, too. I was at a very low point in my life. It reminded me of the pain I felt when my father passed, only the pain was different. It hurt just as bad, but in a totally different way. Going to work was difficult because he was there and I had to see him. By mid-October my weight and moods were very visible. I was depressed and couldn't stop crying, whether I was in the shower, bathroom, my car, at work, wherever. I felt myself hitting rock bottom.

Nevertheless, I began to write in my journal again. I prayed more. I didn't sleep much, but when I did, I cried myself to sleep and woke up crying. The more I cried, the harder I prayed. I would cry until I hyperventilated.

One day during a crying spell, I begin to pray.

I told God exactly what I wanted. I don't remember really telling Him anything. *Who am I to tell my Master anything?* I thought. That day, I said, "God I don't want to feel this way, anymore. If this is the man you have for me, bring him back to me. If not, take him away. Take away all these feelings I have, 'cause I don't want them anymore. I don't wanna feel this way. God, I'm not asking you. I'm telling you."

I remember praying that prayer out loud and walking back-and-forth in my apartment. The day after that, I was flipping through the Bible and came across a scripture in Proverbs 3:5-6. It reads, "Trust in the Lord with all your heart and lean not on your own understanding. In all your ways acknowledge him and he will make your paths straight." I'm sure I'd heard that verse before, but it didn't really mean anything to me then.

At that moment, it meant everything to me. I highlighted it in my bible and read it over-and-over again. In the meantime, my recent ex's relationship with the other girl flourished. Whenever I felt weak, I recited that bible verse. I cried less and started to eat again. I completely gave it to God, even though He already had it. In my heart, I let it go.

Fast-forward to 2010. His relationship with her was still flourishing. They're planning to get married in March of 2011 and I'm invited to the wedding.

We are all friends. It wasn't an easy journey, but God led, so it was a destined journey. When he stood in my apartment nearly a year after we had broken up and told me that he was going to propose to his new girlfriend, all I could do was be happy for him. That's what God would have wanted. That's what you do when you love someone.

Yes, I still love him and a part of me will always love him. However, I love him enough to let go and allow him to be happy with the woman that God put in his life. Some people are put in our lives for a season. He served his season and I learned a lot about me, relationships, and listening to God. If He only put this man in my life to show me how to appreciate a good man, I am thankful.

Thank You, Lord, for showing me the hard way. Thank You for letting me know that when You put someone in my life, I am not to look anywhere else, no matter what. I heard Him loud and clear and I ignored him, but I thank Him for being so forgiving.

See, ladies, I failed the first test, but please believe that I'm prepared for the next. God doesn't make mistakes and I don't question His will in my life. Again, I say, "Trust in the Lord with all your heart and lean not on your own understanding. In all your ways acknowledge Him and He will make your paths straight."

Shaka is a journalist and freelance writer. She graduated from Clark Atlanta University with a

Bachelors of Arts in journalism. She enjoys writing, cooking and spending time with her family and friends in her spare time. Shaka is pursuing her aspiration to become a lawyer and currently lives in Georgia.

They Need Us

By Ashley M., *Engaged*

I met my fiancé when we were both still very young and full of energy. I was 18 and he was 20. It's been a tough journey, but what I respect most about him is that he never misled me. He never led me to believe that he was ready for a committed relationship when he was in fact, not ready. Most of our time getting to know each other led us to being good friends, and he made it very clear that was what it was about.

He was my friend, and was honest and just not ready...for 5 years. But I loved him. So I waited. While waiting and being on-and-off with him, I dated other guys. I worked hard. I grew into myself and enjoyed every minute of it. I enjoyed discovering who I was, while embracing my flaws. I enjoyed discovering what I would and would not tolerate in a relationship. I enjoyed the spiritual connection that I grew with God. It wasn't about anything or anyone else.

I dated other guys, but they couldn't even come close to having the effect on me that my current fiancé did. They could care less about who I truly was beneath the surface. They were just nice guys.

My fiancé is now my best friend. Neither of us were brought up in the church, nor do we center our relationship around religion. We're spiritual people. We try to become better each day, and we desire to learn more about different religions. However, we knew that if we were to get married it would be necessary to talk to someone about the challenges we face.

Our premarital counselor taught us a number of things about being young, married and staying in faith. This is the one lesson that will always remain close to me.

In Genesis 2:18, the LORD God said, "It is not good for the man to be alone. I will make a helper suitable for him." Our pastor translated this to say that a man *needs* you. His exact words were, "I wish that Christian women would understand that a man needs them, and then they would stop chasing men." I'm not sure why it happens, but we as women, tend to devalue ourselves by chasing after men and making excuses. Many of our men are not taught to respect and honor women, but we continue to perpetuate this.

Ladies, just know that he needs you. I know that my fiancé needs me! Ha! I know that the small details in life would slip through the cracks if I weren't there. I know that he needs my friendship, support, and inherent qualities to compliment him. We all need to remind ourselves of this often.

My words of wisdom would be that being single is truly a time meant for growth. It's a much better time when spent focusing on yourself as opposed to chasing after a man. While men sometimes take longer than we'd like to "pop the question," the time that we can spend learning to value ourselves and grow faith in God is truly something to hold on to. It will always serve as a reminder to just how fabulous we are alone and how we are indeed a compliment to a man's life.

Ashley M. is the President of Medley Incorporated, Special Promotions Manager for Jones Magazine, and a graduate of Texas Southern University. She is a self-proclaimed nerd and a lover of all things high-fashion, tech, and media.

Beyond this Journey

By Yvonne, *Divorced*

*"Fear not [there is nothing to fear], for I am with you;
do not look around you in terror and be dismayed, for I
am your God. I will strengthen and harden you to
difficulties, yes, I will help you; yes, I will hold you up
and retain you with My [victorious] right hand of
rightness and justice."*

- Isaiah 41:10

This is the Rhema word from God that
resonated in my soul and spirit when I found myself
"single again" after being married for 22 years. It's
His powerful words that strengthened and sustained
me during a very difficult period in my life. I felt
alone, abandoned, and completely betrayed by the
man I thought was my "knight in shining armor," my
"happily ever after prince," so to speak. To me, this
was the hardest walk I had to face in my adult life. It
seemed easier to escape or run away than to deal
with the heart wrenching reality of a life that would
eventually lead to 7 years of stifling illnesses. You see,
I not only had to allow God to heal my broken heart
and restore my well-being, but I had to learn what
true forgiveness was really all about. This was my
journey on discovering what real love meant and how

to love even the "seemingly unlovable" from the world's perspective.

If I say that I am truly His child, my focus must be to please my loving Heavenly Father above any other desire in my life. This was easier said than done and meant dying to myself daily and allowing the Holy Spirit to take complete control of my life. I was gently reminded of Galatians 2:20, which says, "I have been crucified with Christ; it is no longer I who live, but Christ lives in me; and the life I now live in the flesh I live by faith in the Son of God, who loved me and gave Himself for me." To sum it up in one word: surrender!

I could hold on to the past and continue to allow myself to wallow in self-pity, regret, and become bitter, or I could allow God to take me on a new journey toward healing, wholeness, and total freedom. It's during this journey that I learned how much the Father truly loved and accepted me just as I was. That's not all. He loved me more than enough to leave me in that devastating state to teach what it means to be totally committed and sold out to Jesus.

As you imagine what my journey was like, know that I am a satisfied woman who has only begun to live a life of love, victory, freedom, and contentment in a Heavenly Father who promises never to leave me nor forsake me. Ladies, His love for you is a pure, holy, guaranteed, and surefire winner because it will quench even the thirstiest of souls for love.

The Journey

The Lord leads, I follow.
Sometimes it's a hike over rocky terrain where it takes
all that is within me to take another step as I hold on,
gripping the end of the rope to keep from slipping,
falling,
and completely giving up.
Other times, it's a stroll thru a field of Texas
wildflowers where I bask in the beautiful sunshine of
His glory and I think to myself, It just doesn't get any
better than this.
Sometimes the storm rages all around me and never
seems to end and I find myself shouting, "Is it morning
yet?"
Other times, I soar so high above the turbulence that
all I sense is His great presence leading me onward to
an awesome victory.
Sometimes, the pressure is so intense that I feel as if I
am about to explode and my eyes begin to weep
uncontrollably from the intense heat.
Other times it's a waltz in the throne room with the
Lover of my soul as the music plays softly as He
whispers words of love that drown out each-and-every
sorrow.
Sometimes the pain is so deep that I feel as if my heart
will break into tiny little pieces, never to be whole, and
beat to the heartbeat of His rhythm again.
Other times, I rest in a deep sweet sleep, filled to
overflowing with a peace that is unexplainable because
I know the Lord watches over me.
Sometimes darkness surrounds me. Am I lost? Am I
forsaken?
His light breaks forth through the darkness revealing
the radiance of the noonday sun all the time.
The Lord speaks, I listen.

The Lord leads, I follow.
A puppet on a string, you may say.
No my friend, quite contraire...
You see my Lord is writing the greatest love story ever told upon the tablets of my heart that will lead to a life of greatness and eternal reward.
It's a romance of my soul that brings healing and wholeness where His pure love can pour through me and encourage others along the way.
His journey brings out the most beautiful array of colors that reflect His glory and a heart of compassion that sees beyond the masks and reaches into the depths of one's soul forever, changing the course of destiny.
The journey.
Our journey.
Lead on my Father, I willingly surrender.

Yvonne
Daughter of the Most High God and Minister of the Gospel of Jesus Christ
To God be the glory!
April 30, 2010

Yvonne is the Administrative Assistant to the Pastor of Missions at Sugar Creek Baptist Church and a Licensed Realtor. She enjoys writing, sewing, and teaching the word of God, as well as mentoring young ladies according to Titus 2. Her favorite pastime (in all the world) is spending time with her four girls and my baby grands. She graduated from Bauder Fashion College with a degree in fashion design/fashion show production.

What I Feel

By Nicole, *Free*

In my head, I'm the poster child for the *Finally Happy with Me* campaign. I've held this position, with some minor slip ups, for the past two years and it is an extremely peaceful place to be! Nevermind how others may label me: "Christian," "businesswoman," "Black/African-American," "thick chick," or "single." I'm making a conscious effort to live and create my own labels. This has been a process and getting to this place included me dealing with three main issues: wholeness, self-worth, and letting go. Today, *happy* is the most important label to me. I've learned that the ones others give don't define me or my character. It's only the ones I write that really matter.

Previous immaturity had me believing that my identity was a part of my romantic relationships. I've had two serious, long-term relationships and when they ended you would've thought that my life ended as well. In hindsight, that shows me that I used the other person to try to complete me, rather than seeking someone to compliment an already whole and happy individual. I understand now that a relationship does not summarize or break me, nor does it control whether or not I will live a happy, fulfilled life. This period of discovery also helped me to realize that happiness truly is a state of mind.

We must control what we allow to affect us. As Christians, we know that the mind is our greatest battlefield which is why the bible reminds us to have the mind of Christ Jesus (Philippians 2:5) and to control our thoughts which ultimately transfer to actions. You may not be able to recite it verbatim, but we've all certainly heard the Proverbs 23:7 (AKJV) scripture which reads, "For as he thinks in his heart, so is he: Eat and drink, said he to you; but his heart is not with you [but is grudging the cost]." The first half of that scripture is the rule. The second half is an example of the rule; it shows how thoughts transfer to action. While you might be saying, "Eat, drink, enjoy," in your heart, you might be having a fit over how much the bill is going to cost at the end of the night. You may not really enjoy yourself at all. We've got to check and cleanse our hearts daily! A huge part of being whole is being set free from negative, controlled thinking. Once we conquer this, we set the foundation for God to fulfill all the desires of our hearts.

Once you desire, you have to believe for it, right? As much as I've grown to love me for me and continue to desire a romantic relationship (and eventually, marriage), it wasn't until very recently that I realized something in my head was telling me that I didn't deserve a husband. Deep down, I believed the lie. Mark 9:24 shares a father's angst and we hear him cry out to God saying, "I do believe, but help me overcome my unbelief!" That helped me so much because it reminded me that I wasn't alone in not believing all the time. Yes, I believe in God, He is my everything, but my lack of belief for those things I desire pointed out a struggle in believing my own worth. Sometimes we've got to remind ourselves that we were created in His image, therefore we are worth all the good in the world.

It's often much easier for us to encourage our girlfriends. We'll say, "You're better than that." "You deserve better." "Don't sell yourself short." "You are worthy of God's best." But do we believe the same for ourselves? I've been speaking to the lie of "You're not worthy" ever since that day because I know that I am worth the desires of my heart. Jesus says so. "Therefore I say to you, What things soever you desire, when you pray, believe that you receive them, and you shall have them" (Mark 11:24 AKJV).

Putting God first, appreciating who you are and believing that you're worth all you desire means you are well on your way to living more than a *super single life*, but a healthy balanced one!

The last major hurdle I experienced in reaching my happy place was a fear of "letting go." I tried so hard to hold on to the past and make things and people 'fit,' rather than just letting them be. I decided that if I really trust God, I will trust His timing and trust that—in regards to my husband—He is preparing someone special just for me. I stopped focusing on what I don't have and started enjoying all that I do have: family, great friends, an exciting career, and many more beautiful things on the horizon.

Know this: You don't have to hold on to anything because your future is far greater than you could ever imagine (Jeremiah 29:11). You just have to be willing to fully let go. We can't walk into the future with even just one foot in the past.

Whether you are unmarried, divorced, engaged, widowed, or dating, learning to love and enjoying yourself is the groundwork for a happy life. Don't be afraid to face your issues and work through them. Understand that whatever you're dealing with, you are not alone—despite how you may feel.

Everyone has insecurities and hardships. God places some of them in us and in our lives so that we can tackle them and become stronger. While I once let romantic relationships dictate my happiness, today, my spiritual relationship is the one that reflects who I truly am. And that's happy.

Nicole studied at the College of Mount Saint Vincent and enjoys listening to music. She is determined to make positive choices in her church and community.

Staying Positive

By Jenna, *Free*

Are you growing tired of being single? Have you been single for a long while now— months, years, and Sundays? Have you prayed for a mate, but it still seems like it's taking forever? Do you find yourself fighting to be genuinely happy for others relationships, engagements, or marriages? Do you read the Bible and still believe that your Boaz is on his way? Do you get constant questions about when are you going to get married and have kids? If you have answered yes to most of these questions, then you are in the same singles boat that I've been rowing in. Yes, this journey through Singles Land has been hard and has it's up-and-down moments, but I still believe there is hope. I still believe that there is someone out there that God has designed just for each-and-every one of us.

I have experienced quite a bit of heart break and feelings of being used and abused. It seems like in my 25 years or since 2004, I've been on this emotional roller coaster with men. Every man that I've come in contact with has had ulterior motives mostly dealing with the physical— sex.

I wanted to be loved and held and I think that that's why I met these types of men and allowed myself to continue to fall into sin. If you have done the same thing or have slipped up again, remember that you can always ask God for His forgiveness and can get back up and try again. Don't let anyone make you feel less of a person because you made a mistake. That's what mistakes are there for: to make them, learn from them, and try not to continue making the same ones.

I think I was desperate for a relationship, instead of being desperate for God. One thing about the Lord is that He is always there with open arms. He chastens those He loves. Seek Him first and all else shall be added. Sometimes being single does bring the feeling of loneliness. However, I remind myself that I have family, friends, and church family who love me and think that I am an awesome young woman. Being alone doesn't have to mean lonely because, on top of all the people that love me, I have God who loves me most of all!

I cried in the past, but knew and still know that through the tears, I had to push forward and be encouraged. I know God has a plan for me. He also has a plan for you as you read this. He has a plan for us all and we have to encourage ourselves sometimes. Push forward and remain patient.

There is a scripture that describes what love is. 1 Corinthians 13:4-7 reads, "Love is patient, love is kind. It does not envy, it does not boast, it is not proud. It is not rude, it is not self-seeking, it is not easily angered, it keeps no record of wrongs. Love does not delight in evil, but rejoices with the truth. It always protects, always trusts, always hopes, always perseveres."

This keeps me grounded and optimistic about love. Don't be surprised if and when love finds you and it is not wrapped in the package that you think it should be in. Don't look in the rear-view mirror and stare back at the past. Leave it behind you and keep moving forward. Stay positive, keep God first and live your life to the fullest. Love is out there and will strike when you least expect it!

Jenna is a fashion designer. She graduated from Clark Atlanta University with a B.A. in fashion design/merchandising. Her hobbies include, but are not limited to writing, poetry, sketching, roller skating, reading, and sewing. She aspires to travel soon.

A Rose from Ashes

By Nichele, *Coupled*

Oscar was intelligent, handsome, attentive, a generous lover, and strong. He was a gentleman that was proud to introduce you to his mother. This was the "honeymoon" stage where he introduced me to his "representative," showing only his positive qualities.

A year into our relationship, pregnancy had taken its toll on my body. Oscar begged me to relax and not work. At night, I would find myself alone with nothing to hold, but my growing belly. Restless, I discovered condoms and pictures of women in his wallet. I uncovered inconsistencies in his work schedule.

One evening, I caught Oscar leaving a woman's apartment when he was scheduled to work. I presented my evidence and countered his explanations. Enraged, Oscar denied nothing and informed me of his new relationship. He proudly replaced me and planned to move her in, offering me the options of a homeless shelter, my car, or living with my mother. I had no job, no money, my mother lived over 200 miles away, and the homeless shelters could not accommodate me.

Oscar promised that I would be leaving his place as he knocked me to my knees. He picked me up by my neck and began chocking me, placing his thumbs in the sink of my neck. As I attempted to release myself, Oscar ranted, "Die, b**ch, die!" He then tossed me out of the house. Stumbling to my car, I noticed that I was blocked in. Oscar struck me until he realized that we drew a crowd and fled.

I felt pain in my back and abdomen with hemorrhaging. While in route to the police, I spotted Oscar waiting at a nearby stop sign with his lights off; he rushed me head on. Making it safely to the police, they documented the evidence of a domestic altercation and escorted me to the hospital. Nurses ran tests and monitored us. For hours, it was touch-and-go, but the baby and I improved over the weekend. That Monday, I went home to find Oscar and his new girlfriend. At that point, my car had become my shelter. My friends referred me for a job and became my support. I obtained an order of protection which allowed me access to our apartment.

Months later, Oscar was notified that his father and step-mother were found dead in their home—a murder-suicide. Oscar inherited a lump sum and his father's possessions. Though his son was due within weeks, he offered no support. My mother soon passed from complications of Multiple Sclerosis and God used her to preserve my family, which gave us a new start.

Oscar's abuse cost him nine months in the penitentiary. As 2 Samuel 22:3 states, "The God of my rock; in him will I trust: [he is] my shield, and the horn of my salvation, my high tower, and my refuge, my saviour; thou savest me from violence." God protected me by sending him away. During Oscar's incarceration, I was spiritually and physically cleansed, renewed and restored. Once released, he attempted to repeat the cycle of violence in my life, but was unsuccessful. I refused to continue our relationship. As a result, our son has suffered the consequences of an absentee father that has petitioned to relinquish his parental rights. Oscar's life began to spiral downhill as he continued his drug and alcohol use and promiscuity, which ultimately led him to contract HIV.

I am abundantly blessed to be free of diseases, afflictions, and addictions. Now, Oscar sees a queen that he couldn't break that is focused on God. He sees a woman pursuing greatness in all that she does and prospering without his support.

God has ordered my steps into a new state where possibilities have been revealed and a new love has emerged. I have experienced love in ways that I never knew were possible. I now understand what it feels like to have someone to love you not for what you can do for them, but because of the light in you. God led me to read Proverbs 31 and identified me as a virtuous woman. Verses 25-26 state, "Strength and honour are her clothing; and she shall rejoice in time to come. She openeth her mouth with wisdom; and in her tongue is the law of kindness." I endured abuse that could have cost me my life, but now, I rejoice in Jesus because wisdom lives in me. I am counted as part of the Blessed 55% because 45% don't make it out of an abusive relationship alive!

Nichele is a single parent of two young men and a recruitment specialist for a healthy relationships program. She is a graduate of the University of Arkansas at Little Rock where she received a Bachelor of Social Work. She loves writing, reading, and spending time with loved ones. She currently resides in Syracuse, NY.

Snatch-and-Restore

By Chanté, *Free*

When I first thought about being single, I choked. This is something I am struggling with even now. I have desired to marry for a while now. I have realized that being a single Christian woman has its many ups and downs. Being single happens to go in both directions for me. Let me start by introducing myself before I take you on the journey I've experienced while being single.

Greetings!

My name is Chanté. You would think one would love to be single, considering the divorce rate! For me, it can be quite intense, since most of my friends are either in relationships or married. I log onto Facebook and get overwhelmed by the many individuals who are single and lonely or are in relationships, yet still lonely. I thought that being in a relationship eliminates you from being lonely. I guess I was wrong.

Being single and lonely are two separate things. The definition of single is "not married," according to Webster's Dictionary. The definition of lonely is being without company. Being single is not just a title, but a state of mind. I had to learn the difference and it was difficult. A dear friend of mine asked me why I wouldn't post that I am single on

Facebook and I laughed and said that I am not trying to date anyone on Facebook because many assume that it is a free e-Harmony. I had no idea that I was struggling with simply acknowledging my singleness. After much consideration and prayer, I finally published that I was indeed single and satisfied. Believe it or not, it felt really good! I had a lot of thinking to do regarding what being single really meant.

As Christians, we are taught to be whole prior to entering into a relationship. For me, being whole is developed through singlehood. God promises through His word to never leave us nor forsake us in Hebrews 13:5. This is a promise that cannot return void, which means that it has to come to pass. Since God promises to never leave us or forsake us, then we should never feel lonely. Trust, this assurance is gained through the process of accepting that you are single, just not alone.

Being single is a great place as long as you have the right focus. There is nothing wrong with desiring a mate or marriage. Just make sure your focus is on the right person, such as God, and not the desire, which would be marriage. Matthew 6:33 instructs us to seek ye first the Kingdom of God and his righteousness and all these things will be added unto us. In my Taffi Dollar voice, "You over here focused on the things rather than God and his kingdom." Here is an awesome quote my friend reminds me, "I don't just want the tangible things God has for me (blessings), but I want the things God has for me to do as well (to be a blessing).

God had to snatch-and-restore me back in proper position with Him. It is not that God does not want to bless us; He just wants to assure that we maintain the blessings. Trust, there is nothing more tragic than receiving a gift and destroying it prior to really enjoying it. Singlehood is the process to assure that when God does bless us (put the blessing on us, not just give us our desires), we are able to maintain the blessing. Take your focus off the fact that you are not yet in a relationship and focus on Him who will not only bless you with a mate, but will bless you to *be* a mate! Remember this: God did not promise an easy flight, just a safe landing.

Enjoy singlehood.

Love and Blessings,

Chanté

Chanté is in pursuit of a B.A. in business administration and enjoys the blessing of being Super Mom. She calls herself a "typical Cali lady" and loves God, people, and life.

The Love Letter

By Min. Neichelle, *Coupled*

a. Luke 1:38, 46-56: my magnificat

"Here am I, the servant of the Lord; let it be with me according to your word."

There was a time in my life when these words were my white flag, my surrender to surrender.

the words I spoke when I raised my hands in defeat and in the deepest pain from wanting to be loved.

trying to do things my way.

I stopped trying,

and I noticed that Black people loved one another in some very unique ways.

I started remembering how people never really *committed* to each other in college;

most people were "talking," "chillin," "kickin' it," all of which could have meant a myriad of different things,

girls would get wrapped up, boys would walk away,

and by the end of college, some of the sweetest girls I knew had become transformed

by hardened hearts, sick bodies, unplanned pregnancies.

       I still see much of this today, and i can't help but to connect this love-issue to the history that lingers in our bodies. how is the notion that one woman is a jump-off and one is wife-material not a reconfiguration of the house-slave/field-slave motif that got us in the beginning of our time here? Is it not the modernization of the idea that one woman is more desirable because of

how much "home training" she's had,

how good she will look in front of his company,

how "too good" she is to break her back in the scorching heat.

Meanwhile, the other one is the one he leaves to fend for herself when she finds herself loving him,

she settles for her place on the periphery of his life,

in the darkness of his bedroom,

where he enters her

and then forces her back onto his periphery until he's ready to see her again.

then, in graduate school in Connecticut, I noticed the way that white people just committed to each other,

left and right, all around, young and old.

They're always together, booed up, openly expressing love to one another.

getting engaged, getting married, having babies born into loving homes.

i even tried to be with a white male, but discovered that my preferences are tied to my hopes for Black men and my honor for Black folks loving other Black folks.

like Mommy and Daddy.

like my Nanny and Papa.

and then he came.

i wasn't met with an angel announcing his presence; he was angelic enough.

i didn't have a chance to get my house in order like Mary did as she awaited Jesus,

> he was either going to love me as I was or
leave me alone.

to my surprise, he loved me.

he loved me with time almost two years ago

> time that he took to understand me

how I fell in love with God and hoped to be a good minister

how I was too jaded to think too far into the future or to imagine myself as a mother

he loved me with time

dancing

eating

talking

sleeping

driving and musing over the beauty of the earth

immersing ourselves in the Bay Area Sunlight

kissing.

And then he came. He was brought to me. magnificently. graciously.

a love letter from God.

the way that I know that my heart is still properly functioning.

And now these words

"Here am I, the servant of the Lord; let it be with me according to your word."

Are my invitation to God to keep healing me

To keep loving me

Teaching me

Showing me myself

And using a humble man to do it.

Like when he asked, "if one of our children brought
home a white person and said that they were in love
– like you love me and I love you – will you love them
less?

I had to *selah*,

see that I couldn't answer the question

and receive there is work to be done.

Yet I realize

That the realization is from God.

God, who steps into our fragmented conditions

And pieces us together.

God, whose hands design one path from two.

two paths from distances so distant

That nearness feels that much better

And feels like God is closer that She was
before.

God, who smiles in the consistency of my beloved's love

and dances in his kisses.

God, who reverses memories of rejection and abandonment,

 once bound in my bones,

 now tumbling from my lips in testimony.

By Min. Neichelle

Taken from *"luke: deeper into healing"*

my final project prepared for Race, Tribe and Hue in the New Testament

Yale Divinity School

Spring 2010

Min. Neichelle is from Texas and loves her family. She graduated from Clark Atlanta University as well as the Yale Divinity School. She believes in a real, vast, and loving God.

Under Construction

By Vonda, *Free*

"Therefore everyone who hears these words of mine and puts them into practice is like a wise man who built his house on the rock. The rain came down, the streams rose, and the winds blew and beat against that house; yet it did not fall, because it had its foundation on the rock. But everyone who hears these words of mine and does not put them into practice is like a foolish man who built his house on sand. The rain came down, the streams rose, and the winds blew and beat against that house, and it fell with a great crash."

-Matthew 7:24-27 (NIV)

Building the foundation of your house is one of the most important tasks when building your home. If the foundation is not properly laid, the entire edifice will be unstable. As I think of the way we live our lives, I think about the things we go through in life. Could our life mistakes be determined by the strength of our foundation? I tell many from time to time, "I'm under construction." More times than less, I get looks as if some may not understand when I use the phrase, "under construction." There are things that I have done in my past life that I knew weren't the paths for me to take until the day I decided to allow God to guide me.

I was really walking on shaky ground while living my life for the moment. Just because it feels good does not mean it's good for you. I found myself indulging in a lifestyle of one which I went seeking. "Seek and ye shall find," is a very true statement. I thought that at a young age this thought would pass as I got older. No, the thought of being in a relationship with the same sex was a thought that remained in my head. So with this thought maturing, it was a thought I had no plans of acting on.

I thought that maybe this was the way I was born. I didn't really act on my thoughts until I was twenty-eight years old. So the search of something I thought was for me was not hard to find. I found myself making excuses to be in places I knew was not the place God wanted me to be. As years passed, I made this lifestyle something that was a part of who I was. This is what I would tell anyone who questioned my way of living. I never had an interest in dressing like a young man or making my features look as if I was a man. Some may say I can be a little tomboyish sometimes because I don't see myself as the type of woman who hates to get dirty. I prefer to dress comfortably rather than be overdressed and not the least bit comfortable.

When I started to date women, I made it a point to date women who looked as such. One being I didn't think it would draw a lot of attention to me if I was with someone who could pass off as a best friend, a buddy, or colleague. I was not interested in the opposite sex, so with that being said I had no desire to be with a woman who looked of the opposite sex. Deep down I knew that this was not the life God wanted for me because when I went out to dinner with the person I was dating, sometimes I would refuse to show any type of male/female attraction. I never thought it was fair to display my lifestyle to others when out in public.

I have never been in agreement with same sex marriage, so after years of treating my flesh with excessive leniency and indulging into lust, I questioned myself one day after getting home from work. It was a day that I will never forget. I asked myself, *Why is it that I have such a love for the same sex?*

As I got myself together to retire from a long day, this thought went through my mind the whole time. I sat on the floor with my back against the closet door. (It's funny how they use the phrase "coming out of the closet.")

I went into deep thought of why I felt this way. I asked myself, *What am I getting out of this lifestyle?* My first thought was that I loved the attention given from the same sex. The first thing that attracted me to a woman was her compassion for me and others. I thought to myself, *Is this something I went without in the past? Something I longed for from someone who I thought should have given it to me without a thought?* The answer was yes to both questions. I was looking for something in someone that I didn't get at a younger age. I knew that once I asked God these questions. They were on my mind for quite some time. I also knew that I had to step away from the lifestyle that I had put so much into. I felt so empty and incomplete and kept trying to fill a void.

I became very tired of being in the company of individuals who sought to find the one thing that would bring them much needed peace. I thought, *Sometimes you have to let go to gain the peace you desire.* After living several years in homosexuality, I finally decided to have a conversation with God. I asked God to remove whatever was not of Him out of my life. I must admit that I was a little afraid to do so because I had invested so much into the lifestyle that I made it a big part of my life. I had surrounded myself around women who were also into homosexuality and thought that if I told them that I had mixed thoughts about the lifestyle, they wouldn't want to be my friends anymore.

The thought to gain something means that you sometimes have to give up something. I took the plunge to find the peace that I desired. I asked God again with a clear mind to remove whatever was not of Him out of me. I have heard many say, "You have not because you ask not."

The day that I asked God to remove whatever is not of Him from me was the day that I decided to remove myself away from homosexuality. That meant that there would be no sitting on the phone and holding conversations with women that I knew would only be temptation. I removed myself away from places that I knew were no good for me.

I found myself feeling so alone at times. I felt so alone that I wanted to return to the lifestyle that I had gotten to know so well. I had times where I wanted to talk to someone to be reassured that I was making the right decision. Deep down inside, I knew that I was making the best decision I ever made.

I made up my mind to go through whatever was needed to rid myself of the lustful spirits that had become a very familiar part of me. I no longer needed a phone because the phone that once would ring nonstop started to ring about three times a day. I would sit and ask myself, *Why have my friends stop calling? Why does it seem as if I have no one to go through this with?*

I realized that *friends* stand by your side when you make positive changes in your life, changes that make you better as a person. I needed to go through that experience. I needed to know that God was always with me. The time came when I understood that I could stand alone without anyone having to hold my hand or telling me that it was going to be ok. I knew then what my flesh needed. It needed to be fed with God's words.

I then started to converse with God as I would with a close friend. I asked Him to guide my path and put me where He wanted me to be. I joined a church and was very pleased with what I was being taught. I found myself wanting to know a person's worth beyond the exterior because sometimes we dress the exterior according to whatever is pleasing to man's eyes.

I remember visiting a gift shop in DC. The gift shop had a large display of the various types of rocks. One rock caught my attention. The reason why this rock caught my eye is because many visiting the gift shop walked past it due to its outer appearance. The rock stood no more than three feet tall in height, so wasn't like the rock wasn't visible, but because the rock had such an unattractive appearance, I decided to ask the sales person if it would be ok for me to take a better look at it. The salesman proceeded to the rock and began to open it to display its inside. I had to take a step back. In disbelief, I had never seen anything so beautiful in my entire lifetime! The rock's wall was pure amethyst. I asked about the price and to my surprise, it was worth five thousand dollars!

The point that I want to make with this story is that the rock was not so attractive by its outer appearance. Its true value was on the inside, where many never took the time to look. I say, "Under construction," because there were things I needed to change about myself that would better me as a person on the inside. In order for me to have a somewhat sturdy life, I needed to start with a sturdy foundation.

Too often, we put ourselves in situations that make it difficult to hear God. With me living my life in homosexuality, I could not hear the voice of God speaking. However, once I removed myself from that lifestyle, I was able to hear Him. I'm not saying that life's a bed of roses when you remove yourself from the sins of the world. From my experience, I think life becomes a battle. It becomes a time when you need to be fully armored.

I would like for everyone that reads my story to know that life is about choices. When you ask God to show you a way out, He will do more and more of His will for our lives. I felt more and more at peace. I would often think of all the people I had met in the past. They all seemed to have everything together on the outside, but were very lonely in the inside. I once told a friend never to look at anyone from the outside to determine their worth. In addition, we must know that our will is not always God's will.

Vonda is a native of Baton Rouge, LA. She now lives in Atlanta, GA, and enjoys volunteering with numerous non-profit organizations. She is a member of Spread the Word Church Ministries.

Reflection of One's Heart:
My Reflection

By Karleata, *Free*

He told me he loved me and no man will ever love me how he did. I was convinced until now. Love can be a disease. It will infect and cause you to lose sight of everything around you, if you let it. Why does love hurt so bad when retrospectively speaking, it was originally supposed to be the purest thing to mankind? It's like I love to love and I hate to love at the same time. It's an oxymoronic statement. I know it is. Everyone desires to be loved, wants to love or *is* in love. I'm single and before I grasped the idea that I could do good by myself, I constantly put myself on discount and settled for less because I didn't know my worth.

Meaningless words are nothing. Nothing is satisfied. Time was wasted.

Sweet nothings were whispered in my ear of promises that never came to pass. Time was being wasted with words of nothing substantial because one person put forth their all and the other ran away with the fact that the other person had fallen. It's a danger when you're in love alone. I've been on blind dates, dates from hell, and dates unexpected. I was a lonely individual at one point in time because I didn't love the fact that being single is a blessing at times. You have the pleasure of dealing and working on yourself spiritually, mentally, and physically. I thought everyone else around me and their love life mattered, when it didn't. When I started to focus on myself that changed my whole life. I've been through the one-night stands, which left me feeling empty and terrible because when everything was said and done, I was still lonely. I felt used.

I've been in relationships with guys that wouldn't make me their woman, but wanted all the benefits of a relationship. They used me. I was lonely and allowed it. Then there were times where I was in a relationship and was unevenly yoked with the individual because we weren't on the same page. He said go left, I said go right. I was up, he was down, I was spiritual and he wasn't. We just didn't work and I ended up lonely again. You have to be careful of getting caught up into wanting a relationship so bad because your friends are in one. They may seem happy when they may not be and you end up compromising.

The best thing you can do is wait. Wait on the Lord for your mate! The Lord knows what you want and need even before you ask Him, so why not wait for God to do it? If you don't, you're going to have to wait for Him to fix it. Sometimes it's good being single because it gives you time to work on you. The bible says, In 2 Corinthians 6:14, "Do not be yoked together with unbelievers. For what do righteousness and wickedness have in common? Or what fellowship can light have with darkness?"

Karleata is a graduate of Erie Community College in Buffalo, NY, and holds a degree in business administration. She is an independent Mary Kay

Beauty Consultant and enjoys reading, writing poetry, playing the guitar, and going to church. She loves the Lord and plans to travel the world. Her motto is: "It's okay to live the lonely leader's road because in the end, you will be happy that you did. You cannot lead from behind."

I Am above the Ruby

By Martha, *Widowed*

"Who can find a virtuous woman? for her price is far above rubies."

-Prov. 31:10

My husband died several years ago. I lost my job (but not my praise!) three years ago when the mortgage industry bottomed out. Since then, I have had a series of short-term, temporary jobs. My two youngest sons are graduating from college this year, which is definitely a blessing from God. Many of my children's teammates, friends, and classmates just happened to assimilate into our family. Whatever their age, religious affiliation (if any), race, or cultural background, they became one of my kids. I am faithful, inquisitive, loving, graceful, cautiously optimistic, and at times, responsibly selfish. I love the Lord and He cares for and about me. The Lord loves and keeps me. I did not always feel this way, however.

I was not always aware of how much He loved me. In personal relationships, I was a giver, nurturer by nature, and generally, it was not reciprocated. I always tried to "fix" him and see the light even in the darkest of situations. I thought that I was the one that could bring out the potential in that man. I could love him into being his best, even when he lied to me, cheated on me, misused me, and emotionally drained me. If only I had just held on a little bit longer. For many years, I was a puppet trying to be everything for everyone. I lost my identity. I almost lost the essence that made me—*me.*

Somehow, I always drew deficient men who needed something: a place to stay, a good meal, a place to rest, or obvious physical comfort. I did not understand the concept of loving myself so I poured my heart and soul into these relationships. If he said he liked blondes, I would dye my hair blonde. If black was his color of choice, black would be the color of my hair. If he liked small women, which I had not ever been, I would practically starve myself and risk illness, trying to be what he—the insignificant man— wanted me to be.

If he did not like the way I dressed, I changed it. If he called at 2:30am, saying he was hungry and missed me, I quickly jumped out of bed, fixed a meal and sat waiting. Sometimes he never showed up. I was good at living in the shadow of someone that did not even have light around them. I was always seeking love and acceptance.

The man that became my husband was what I thought was too good to be true. He was friendly, affectionate, loving, compassionate, and would give a stranger the shirt off his back. However, there was a dark side. He was a Vietnam veteran who suffered from posttraumatic stress disorder and was bipolar. I had no knowledge of either condition until his untimely demise. He was extremely happy for periods of time, while on the other end of the spectrum, was angry, sad, loud, mean, and surly. In spite of the dark side, I loved the man that I saw in him during those good times. However, we eventually had to part and share custody of the children.

Having a habit of attracting emotionally detached men, men who just wanted somewhere to hang around without being committed, I knew that I was unfulfilled and not being the woman of God that He wanted me to be. I prayed, fasted, prayed, fasted, and prayed some more. How many of you know that the devil will throw you into a frenzy when he knows that you are trying to get your spiritual life together?

I started meeting some of the finest, sweetest brothers a sister could want in her life. They were from a range of ages, complexions, big pretty smiles, and charm that you would not believe! All of a sudden, my phone was ringing off the hook with men who wanted to "hook up." I prayed for discernment and deliverance.

I soon could not get too comfortable in the churches I visited. There were too many cliques, backbiting, doctrinal issues, and internal fighting that tormented me. If you were not born into a particular church, you and your family never quite fit in, no matter how many organizations you joined, tithes you paid, or contributions you made. I was already sinking in sand. I did not need more confusion. How many of you know that God is a solid rock, a solid foundation? I had to stop looking and start listening.

The spirit speaks to us, but sometimes we are too loud to hear it. It is so important to have quiet time with the Father. He can refresh, renew, and rejuvenate you. In the past three years, I lost jobs, my home, and could not help pay for my boys' college expenses. God provides! I pray and I listen. I meditate on His word. I talk to Him daily about everything. He guides me. He loves me. I find the ultimate fulfillment in His presence. It is so hard to describe. I feel safe, loved, and kept by God. I ask for His guidance in all situations. "Trust in the Lord with all thine heart, lean not unto thine own understanding" (Proverbs 3:5).

When I recall my losses, my home, relationships, jobs, material possessions, I realized that my gains are phenomenal. *God is my all-in-all.* I know the anxiety of not knowing where you will sleep or if you will have a meal. I watched so called friends scurry from me when I lost my home, didn't answer my phone calls, and avoided me whenever they could. A couple of times I told a few, "You act like you think I am going to ask you if I can come live with you. Don't worry. I don't want anything from you."

I saw the stress and concern in my son's eyes when he asked, "Where we gonna live, Momma? Where will I come home to on holiday breaks?" Uncertainty was our companion, but the Lord was my stanchion. *My God is a keeper!* I knew He did not bring me this far to desert me. Then I was diagnosed with diabetes and hypertension, with no insurance. *My God is a deliverer.* I found a way to get the health care that I needed.

God has truly embraced me, enriched my life, and led me to a church home. He has changed my outlook on life. I now know my value as His creation, His child. He is my provider, my keeper, my best friend, doctor, lawyer, and comforter. In Him, I am neither too short or tall, nor am I too heavy or thin. It does not matter what color my hair is, nor does it matter what size my clothes are. I do not need another person to validate me. I don't have to compromise my values to be accepted by a man. I do not have to be a member of a clique, and I do not have to drive the biggest, most expensive car. I don't have to live in the biggest house or possess a particular bank account. I am accepted just as I am.

I may encounter valleys in life, but I know that there is a Lily in the Valley. I may have some hills to climb, but I know that He is beside me. I've found a resting place. I can call Him anytime, as many times as I need to. I get comfort in calling on the name of Jesus. My Father loves me unconditionally and knows my every need. He is refining and perfecting me, so that I will shine as the virtuous, dynamic, blessed woman that I am destined to be.

With the Lord beside me, I am positioned for greatness. Everything that I needed and desired, I found it in Him. If He decides that there is a man that He wants in my life, He will cause our paths to cross. If not, I am still blessed to be kept by God.

Martha is a single, blessed woman of God. She is a grandma, nana, sister-girl, aunt, friend, and confidant. She is currently attending college as a journalism major. She describes herself as a "five-time, natural mother and a hundred-time adoptive mother."

Single's Refinery

By Wendy, *Free*

"They that wait upon the Lord shall renew their strength. They shall mount up on wings as eagles. They shall run and not be weary, they shall walk and not faint."

-Isaiah 40:31

As a single mother of two boys, I have been in the "refiner's fire" of dating for the last eight years of my life. I refer to it as the "refiner's fire" because it is the closest parallel to what God does before He presents a man to his wife. The final stage of gold production, "refining," involves a somewhat tedious process that involves removing impurities that remain present in gold after the smelting process. Refining companies receive doré bars, as well as scrap gold, and re-liquefy the metal in a furnace.

Workers add borax and soda ash to the molten metal, which separates the pure gold from other precious and less precious metals. In this process, all of the metal products that are not pure gold boil to the top of the gold mixture and are skimmed off until all of the boiling contents are pure gold. A sample is then taken to a lab for tests, or assays, that measure the gold content. In most cases, the gold is 99.9 percent pure. Workers then cast the gold produced during refining into bars.

The final step, which is "refining," depends on how the gold will be used. Pure gold is generally too soft for most practical applications, so other metals are nearly always added to it. When gold is combined this way, it forms an alloy. Scientists and goldsmiths often use colors to designate the various gold alloys that are possible. For example, white gold is made by combining gold with nickel, silver or palladium. Red or pink gold is an alloy of gold and copper. Blue gold is the result of mixing gold with iron.

This is similar to the process that God takes us through before He presents us with our mates. We are tried and tested through bad relationships, heartache, experiences, and unexplainable circumstances. In the end, those experiences *refine* and *purify* us so that in the end, we are like pure gold. It is interesting that the purest gold is too soft for formation and requires mixture with another metal. That is our mate. When we allow God to choose our mate, He selects the best compliment to our end result. Genesis tells us that God presents the woman [Eve] to the man [Adam] after Adam has been put to sleep [taken through a process].

I have come to learn that patience is a fruit of the spirit. Patience has to process its perfect work in us as women. In my waiting process, I learned more about myself than those I was in a relationship with. Having still been single, I am involved in a courtship with a God-fearing man who understands my value and appreciates my worth. One thing my mother taught me is the fact that the man for you will recognize who you are and treat you accordingly.

This is more than the truth. We wait for many things. Why not be patient and wait for the man that God has chosen? Take the time. Be processed.

Wendy resides in Atlanta, Georgia. Professionally, she is an expert in perinatal and neonatal nursing in the state of Georgia as well as California. She has endured numerous toxic relationships and has learned to embrace patience. Wendy answered God's call to ministry in Nov 2009, received her ordination as a non-denominational pastor, and is currently active in ministry to men and women nationwide. Wendy hopes to one day build a Christian comprehensive women's health center focused on people of color in an urban inner city.

Hidden Insecurity

By Monique, *Free*

Insecurity is the feeling of not being enough of what God has created you to be. Insecurity will have you wearing interchangeable masks: The mask of *hurt* will have you ignoring people you love because of hurt and bitterness. The mask of *slyness* will have you quiet to your own thoughts that continue to break down your mind. The *mask of anger* will have you angry, frustrated, irritable and crying often. The mask of *jealousy* will open the door for jealousy and covetousness. The mask of *wrath* will cause you to be rude and unglued.

Insecurity remains loyal to its parents: rejection and abandonment. When you are insecure, pleasing people becomes the norm more than pleasing God. The mask of fear will clothe you and can cover you from head-to-toe. It can absorb the mind to the point where you will begin to hide and reject people, change, yourself, and your purpose. Insecurity will prohibit you from giving and receiving love. God will show you a reflection of yourself and offer you a choice to deal with your issues. God's reflection will reveal insecurities that can be hidden well by some of your best tactics and masks, but remember that God knows all and sees all. He wants you to be free of insecurity because it will have you avoiding crowds and social networking. The mask of selfishness is when you will become oblivious to ministry opportunities. Insecurity can lead you into bad decision making. It will hide purpose from you and create a judgmental attitude and irresponsible behavior. Insecurity will also inhibit healing and deliverance from past hurts.

I heard God say, "Come to me, all (ye) that labour and are heavy laden, and I will give you rest" (Matthew 11:28). As single women, it is important that we check ourselves daily and check our insecurities. What is it that you are insecure about or what is it that you are insecure in? There are many components in being whole and one of them is defeating insecurity. Our goal should be to become a whole woman of God. We should not want to walk into an ordained relationship half whole and broken. I do not believe that's the will of God. I believe that God brings two whole people (man and woman) together for holy matrimony so that two wholes can become one heartbeat that is totally depended on Him. It is only through the power of God that one can walk in faith, regarding this matter. We must confront and defeat insecurity and then destroy its parents.

Insecurity will keep you from exploring new opportunities. It will prevent you from looking people in the eyes. It will hinder you from becoming an entrepreneur and everything God said you are. It will also keep you in an unforgiving state and unable and unwilling to forgive yourself and others. It will have you emotional and extra sensitive. It sets high expectations for people to meet that will never happen because they are unrealistic. But insecurity will have you set them anyway, so that one can be comforted by disappointment and confirmation of its parents.

What was it that happened or was done to you that opened the door for insecurity? Take time to discover the root and when you do, uproot it and began to live again through healing and deliverance.

Say to yourself, "God, I am not whole. My mind plays tricks on me and I am battling insecurity. Help me, Jesus, to discover me, so that I may be able to retire the masks. I pray that I may be able to truly be free in you and that I may be victorious in my battle, as I conquer the heads of insecurity knowing that with you, nothing is impossible. So draw me nearer. Nearer, precious Lord, to the place where I first received you. To the place that gave birth to me, free of insecurities in Jesus Name."

Monique is currently an assistant property manager/bookkeeper for campus advantage which manages CAU Suites in Atlanta, GA. She has a Bachelor of Science degree in engineering with a concentration in electrical from Clark Atlanta University in Atlanta, GA. Today, it is her desire and passion to become a pioneer and educator of innovation and serve as a role model to empower women, especially girls, to explore careers in engineering, but most importantly discover themselves in purpose. She intends to focus her career specifically within the electrical field, as she has many visions and goals that will change the world through innovation!

Slow Your Roll and Seek God

By Latausher, *Free*

I always tell people the reasons I'm single and why I don't tolerate certain things in a relationship. When I grew up, coming from a home of 8, I saw how my mother and father's relationship was. My dad was in-and-out of relationships with other women at the time. Seeing my mother being hurt and rejected, led me to tell myself that it would never happen to me.

Marriage is a design created by God. When God gave instructions for marriage, He told Adam to love her [Eve] the way He created her through Him. He said, "Therefore shall a man leave his father and his mother, and shall cleave unto his wife: and they shall be one flesh" (Genesis 2:24). Nothing else matters outside of that.

I knew my father loved my mom, but I saw the pain she went through trying to raise us as he was out doing his own thing. This started my lack of trust. I don't tolerate dishonesty or unfairness, so I found myself in-and-out of relationships over the years. The men I met were not honest, faithful, or truthful.

I was in relationships for the intimacy. I found myself like the lady in the Bible who was at the well. She had 5 husbands. I, too, was in relationships with 5 men. I wasn't intimate with all of them. I was intimate with two and played games with three [I was being safe and I thank God for that]. I didn't really have feelings for them because I said that I wasn't gonna be hurt.

I examined people. I always observed. And when I look back and think of how I listened to their conversations, I could tell where they were.

Out of all 5 of those previous relationships, one remained a close friend, whom I have known for nearly 5 years. He was the last on the totem pole.

I know he is a gentleman, but even with that, I haven't put all the cards on the table. I feel that he needs to show me more. I understand what God says and God will not allow me to be with anyone that will not allow me to do the things He has called me to do.

Being a single woman, I just encourage women to follow the scripture, "Trust in the Lord with all your heart and lean not on your own understanding. In all your ways acknowledge him and he will direct your paths" (Proverbs 3:5-6). The word of God teaches us, "But seek first his kingdom and his righteousness, and all these things will be given to you as well" (Matthew 6:33). When we seek God and his kingdom, we follow his commands and stand in His will. We don't have to look for anything. We may think that some of the guys we run into are the right one, but when God takes the scales off of our physical eyes, we will see everything spiritually.

Before we got into God's realm, we thought the ways we wanted to think. But when we seek God, He allows us to see everything spiritually and not physically, just like with Paul. *You were in darkness, but now you're in the light.* When you're not seeking God, you're in darkness, but when you seek Him, you will be in the light. "Blind" people don't seek God. Therefore, they are lost.

I once was blind, but now I see. Sometimes, God will allow you to see things that you can't and don't wanna see. He will show you that a certain person doesn't have everything together and that's when you delete him out of your life. He is not the one. Delete him from your life. He gotta go. Holla!

We don't need to be anxious or desperate. When women have been alone for so long, they get desperate. When we seek Him, He will give us what we need. He will fix that particular man up just for us.

Sometimes a certain man may not be for you, but because God loves you, he may let you have the desire of our hearts. He will mold, make, shape, and prune that man so that he can become the man that God wants him to be. The book of John talks about how God can prune them.

You can identify a man for the long haul or for a hit-and-run. Hit-and-run men will wanna take you out to dinner, or nowhere, and be anxious to get you in the bed. I don't care how slick a person thinks they are, they will be revealed. Men who want to be there for the long haul are not anxious. Talking about having sex would be the last thing on the agenda. He will ask, *How was your day? Have you eaten today? How do you feel?*

Another thing I have learned is that some single women don't communicate. They just jump into things. They need to learn to communicate to see where men's minds and hearts are. They need to put everything on the table and let them know what they want, all while seeking God for guidance.

I have found that many people find themselves getting married before the man is saved. Sometimes women get saved before men. Sometimes the woman wants to give up because the men are not walking in the will of God. However, God can clean up their mate. So many people marry who they are not supposed to have and don't want to do it anymore, but they must wait and trust God.

Everything you want and can think of, God's got.

Latausher is a mother of four from Atlanta, GA. She is a minister of the gospel and a woman after God's own heart. Her favorite quote: "I'm a kingdom builder, building life for the kingdom. Seeking the least, the last, and the lost." She loves to go on cruises, shop, travel, and spend time with family and children.

Bag Lady

By Andrea, *Free*

"I can do all things through Christ who strengthens me."

-Philippians 4:13

Almost all my life, I've dealt with issues that made impacts on my personality, morals, and how I am as a woman. I've had family issues that ran deep with my immediate- and extended families. They all started from when I was a little girl, no older than 5 years old. Although I have forgiven those individuals, the conflicts have become like extra baggage that I've carried throughout my past.

At the age of 12, I didn't make friends easily. I was chosen and later tossed to the side by some kids because I didn't "fit in." I reached a point where I nearly took my own life, but chickened-out. I thought, *There's got to be a better way.*

Until my high school career, I never found that "better way." I took a turn for the worst in my junior year. Thinking that all hope was lost, I turned against God and found a group of friends that was in my same state of hopelessness. In late January of 2007, I became suicidal again and slit my wrist with no hope of someone on which to rely. This resulted in me taking on more baggage. I called myself a "bag lady." I am grateful to have survived.

At that time in my life, I had a history of molestation, low self-esteem, a low number of reliable friends, and no hope for my future. I participated in a debutante program in my senior year, hoping to rebuild my self-esteem and morals. I wanted to find my true identity. I got my best friend back that year, too. I also helped her to cope with the sudden loss of her mother. When high school ended, my past was behind me, or so I thought.

After the first month of my arrival to Virginia, I lost control of my freedom and allowed things to get out of hand. I let my past and others take advantage of me, including my best friend, who eventually ran away to live with her boyfriend.

Nevertheless, I've learned from my mistakes. God has forgiven me and I'm learning to forgive myself. Today, I have no regrets. I've learned to stand up for myself and I no longer do the things that I used to do. I let no one or anything come between me, my morals, my goals, and God. This is Andrea and I've left my baggage behind.

Andrea resides in Chesapeake, VA, with her mom, dad and sister. She is a member of Pleasant Grove Baptist Church where she is involved with the Young Adult Ministry and the Youth and Young Adult Missionaries. She is also working on getting a bachelor's degree in criminal justice, where she plans to work with juveniles.

The Art of Loving Unconditionally

By Michelle, *Free*

"Do not be overcome by evil, but overcome evil with good."

-Romans 12:21

I'm sure some people wonder why I didn't get an abortion and whether or not I see my rapist's face every time I look into my son's face. I love looking into my son's face and I do so every opportunity that I can. You wanna know why? Because all I see is God's grace, His blessing, and His love for me. I see beauty and I see the future in front of me.

Talk about situational ironies, the man who raped me did a horrid thing and the result was a blessing. If I had not been raised in a Christian household with parents that forgave and taught their kids to forgive those who trespassed against them, I would have probably had an abortion, hated men, hated myself, and maybe even tried to hurt myself out of self-pity, while carrying a sense of unworthiness.

44 years ago, a man was being kicked (literally) out of a church and told to "leave before we call the police." The man with his few belongings and bloody nose did not try to fight back, although he was twice the size of the two men kicking him.

The small crowd that had gathered to watch gasped when they saw a young Caucasian woman saying, "Excuse me," as she pushed her way toward the front to help this poor black fellow. She approached to help him back on his feet.

Long-story-short, the young woman was Shannon Huisemann and the black man was William Woods, both of which are my parents. Their 44 years together were not easy.

My father, who was "uneducated" only had an equivalent of today's 8th grade. My mother was an upper middle-class, first-generation, German American who'd attended college as paid for by her father. She was disowned for her decision to marry my father and that meant she'd receive no more money for school. My dad worked as many jobs as he could to make sure my mother stayed in school. Today, she has a PhD in economics. My dad, on the other hand, claims that if he had bought shares in the Milwaukee Glass Company, he would have been like Bill Gates by now. He said this, considering the number of times he had to buy new windows to replace the ones that were broken by those who hated my parents' relationship.

One time, while leaving work, he suffered a concussion after getting a severe beating. His vehicle was also blown up one time. Thankfully, no one was in it. He suffered broken ribs on a separate beating.

What's amazing is that my folks did not forgive once all the hate stopped. They forgave and prayed for their attackers *each-and-every night.* They taught me the art of forgiving as well as the art of loving unconditionally. My mother did not seek an educated white male from the suburbs within the same socio-economic background as hers. She found a diamond in an "uneducated Negro" without a job. She said that she noticed him glow when she was in the crowd. He had the glow of a Godly man.

My father single-handedly paid in full all of my mother's tuition and even sent my grandfather a check of the amount that he had initially paid in tuition. My mom's dad, in a mix of pride and shame, never cashed the check but framed it! That poor black man from 44 years ago was so "rich" then and still is today. He passed those "riches" to his daughter and son, so with such riches, how can I hate my son or the man who hurt me? We will always be a victim if we don't forgive.

I refuse to be a victim, so I love *now* more than ever.

Michelle is a Christian lady with a brown belt in karate. She is a nurse (MSN) and will be a Certified Registered Nurse Anesthetist (CRNA) this year.

ACKNOWLEDGMENTS

Neely:

Truly, this book would not have been completed without the help of our Lord and Savior, Jesus Christ. I give Him credit for this book. My best friend, Jenna, made a comment at the end of one of my notes on Facebook on super singles. She wrote, "Super singles, activate!" That gave me the idea for the book's title. Thank you, girl, for that.

Thank you, Ms. Tillman, for writing the foreword to this book. Alexis and I agreed on the ideal person.

A special thank you goes to Alexis "Fly" Jones for wanting to join me in this project. I could not find a better, more flexible partner. It was almost too-good-to-be-true.

I am grateful for all of the women who were bold enough to share their stories with complete strangers. You are courageous and awesome for your contributions.

I also give thanks to you, the reader, for taking the time to read this book. Thanks so much for what you're doing. If you would, please share this publication with more women. There are so many ladies that need to know that they are not alone. They hunger for help in their situations. Perhaps you can be that vessel of assistance. This book is meant to motivate women to keep pushing forward in their single, or unmarried, state. It can be a lonely road, but it's doable and has more treasures than we know.

If you would, please extend word of this book to as many women as you can.

I am grateful for you.

Alexis:

I am full of joy and thankful to the King of Kings, our Lord and Savior Jesus Christ, for this book that I believe will bless many women. Thank you to the women that, without hesitation, were willing to share their testimonies for the edification and purpose of building up others. Without you, there would be no *Super Singles, Activate!*

Special thanks to Neely Terrell for your willingness to collaborate and foreseeing the vision. Look at what a conversation via Facebook grew into! Love you lots.

Thanks, Ms. Brenda Tillman, for writing the foreword to this book. Thank you for believing in its message of hope and empowerment.

To my dearest Mom & Dad: Words cannot describe my gratefulness for the love, prayers, and support that you have given me in all my endeavors. I thank God for choosing you as my parents.

To all my family and to friends (both past & present), *thank you*. Without you, I would not be who I am today. I would not be able to continue to be molded by God and walk this path called life.

As a proclaimed Christian that helps build and develop images of my clients to their public by profession, I view it as an honor —my pleasurable duty—to purposefully emulate the image of God and represent Him in everything I do. With that said, the purpose of this book is to encourage, challenge and motivate you, the reader, to hear and wait on the Lord in your season of singleness. In the meantime, take time out to identify who you are in Christ, to love HIM more...to love *you* more.

You are beautifully and wonderfully made (Psalm 139:14). According to God, you were made in *His* image and when *He* saw what *He* had made, *He* saw that is was good... (Genesis 1:27, 1:31).

Be blessed, my beautiful sisters in Christ.

About the Editors

Neely Terrell has always had a passion for creative writing, relationships, and people. One of her main goals was to get aspiring writers published. She's realized that whatever goal she wants to accomplish is reachable because she does all that is necessary to obtain it. Thanks to God, supportive family, friends, and acquaintances, she is encouraged to do everything that she's dreamed. Neely is the author of two books, *Dumped and Delivered: Seeds to Uplift the Brokenhearted, Single, and Committed* and *thebrownorange: My Life in Chapters and Chunks.*

She is an editor, motivator, and school librarian. A native of Atlanta, GA, Neely currently lives in Buffalo, NY.

Contact information:

Facebook.com/Neely.Terrell

Twitter @thebrownorange

Alexis "Fly" Jones can be described as one with the heart of an encourager, a supporter, and an assistant with a prophetic name meaning "helper of mankind." Former relationships that resulted in hard lessons, but an emotional dependency upon God to see her through, led her towards a desire to collaborate on a book that she hopes will encourage women to remain faithful and patient in both love and purpose.

Blessed with a creative mind, and keen communication skills, such has resulted in her becoming a public relations consultant by trade and VP of a brand development company catering to the fashion, arts and entertainment field, thus her brand name "Fly" was derived. Throughout the years, Alexis' vessels of communication have been molded and displayed through her God-given talent in art, writing, networking, and now through her first published book. She currently resides in Houston, TX.

Contact Me: Facebook.com/AlexisFlyJones or follow me on Twitter @alexis_fly

You can contact us both at

supersinglesactivate@gmail.com

11511850R00123

Made in the USA
Charleston, SC
01 March 2012